JAZZ
ARRANGING

JAZZ ARRANGING

NORMAN DAVID
URSINUS COLLEGE

Ardsley House Publishers, Inc., New York, NY

Address orders and editorial
correspondence to:
Ardsley House, Publishers, Inc.
320 Central Park West
New York, NY 10025

ISBN: 1-880157-60-8

Printed in the United States of America

10 9 8 7 6 5 4 3 2 1

With great love,
to my father and mother

CONTENTS

❖❖❖❖❖❖❖❖❖

PREFACE

People grow up acquiring different musical aptitudes and tastes. A person's particular experiences with music styles as well as societal influences will determine significantly how he or she listens to and relates to music. Consequently, gaining technical ability in any area of music will not necessarily guarantee "hip" artistic expression. One does not just feel swing or have soul without regularly experiencing creative music by either listening to it, playing it, or both. This is why a person who has previously embraced jazz and other sophisticated styles of music will often be tuned in instinctively to many of the facets of progressive harmony and arranging prior to studying these subjects formally. Regardless of musical background it is also essential, while advancing in practical skill and intellectual knowledge, to continue maturing in one's *feeling for and appreciation of* creative music.

This text presents an examination of arranging methods and their applications. I have made every effort to explain the information clearly in a logical order, and to compose musical examples that adequately illustrate the material. The text begins with a historical overview of jazz band instruments and a study of their physical and tonal characteristics. This is followed by discussions of relevant terminology, notational devices, and principles of theory. The remainder of the text contains studies of arranging technique for the rhythm section, combinations with up to five horns, larger ensembles, and big band. Each chapter concludes with a series of exercises. The text is designed for use in a jazz studies program and as a professional reference manual for musicians in general.

ACKNOWLEDGEMENTS

I want to express my sincere appreciation to Karyn Bianco for answering many questions and assisting throughout the publishing process and to Laura Jones for her expertise and guidance in the technical aspects of putting the book together.

My original manuscript proposal was reviewed by Ted Pease and Ken Pullig, Berklee College of Music; Tom Boras, New York University; as well as Paris Rutherford, University of North Texas. I appreciate the dedication of these colleagues, and am grateful for their positive reviews and perceptive suggestions for improving the material.

Through the years, I have studied and worked with hundreds of instrumentalists, composers, arrangers, and music educators. I have heard my compositions and arrangements performed live or recorded by world-class players. The inspiration of these gifted people was an invaluable factor in the formulation of this text. Deserving of special mention are the following top-rank musicians and true friends who have consistently encouraged me and have expressed confidence in my efforts: Ben Schachter of Temple University and Bucks County Community College, my great friend and musical ally, who graciously proofread some of the manuscript; Ken Pullig, Chairman of the Jazz Composition Department at Berklee College of Music; Dr. John French, Chairman of the Department of Music at Ursinus College; and Dr. Wayne Schneider, Department of Music, University of Vermont.

INTRODUCTION

Arranging is the practice of *designing* musical works; it follows composition chronologically. Composer and arranger are often the same person.

An arrangement can be described as ensemble music that is planned and diagrammed in advance of performance. Arrangers must be well-rounded musicians with adequate knowledge of composition, theory, and instrumentation.* Their craft is fueled by inspiration and soul power—it involves a sense of daring, spontaneity, and a considerable amount of self-confidence. Here are examples of some of the many questions arrangers must answer in preparing to work:

- What instrumentation will be used?

- How many choruses will there be?

- How will the melody be modified, if at all?

- Which instrument(s) will be assigned the melody?

- Will there be any reharmonization?

- Which instrument(s), if any, will solo?

- Should an introduction be added?

These important questions address only a few of the many cosmetic features that pertain to an arrangement. Furthermore, decisions must be made on technical procedures–voicings, range, backgrounds, section writing, etc.

---

* A person's ability to arrange music must include a strong knowledge of contemporary harmonic theory and practice. In a representative jazz studies program, students may study harmony and arranging concurrently. However, musicians—students and otherwise—should already be adequately comfortable with the fundamental principles of contemporary harmony before undertaking arranging. Although it is inevitable that various aspects of music theory will crop up during the course of discussions, this text is not a theory text. The study has been designed assuming that the reader possesses sufficient basic harmonic knowledge.

This study focuses on jazz ensembles typically seen and heard on stage and offered in college curricula. Thus, some wind instruments, many percussion instruments, and all orchestral strings except the double bass will be excluded from discussions in the text. Orchestral strings are potentially a beautiful addition to any arrangement. Their use, however, is scarce in jazz combos and an expensive proposition in a professional situation. Strings are a luxury usually employed in the recording studio or in large-scale productions. In any event, although it would be possible to apply certain band methods, string writing has its own particular technical demands. Several excellent texts on orchestration are available to the arranger or composer who wishes to examine writing for instruments uncommon to jazz ensembles. (See the Suggested Bibliography at the back.)

Jazz-arranging technique is applicable to all genres of contemporary bands. Consequently, in addition to being knowledgeable about important jazz practice and tendencies, arrangers should also be familiar with other common contemporary music styles. Following are some possible settings:

- A horn section of trumpet, alto saxophone, and trombone could front a jazz combo or back up a rock group.

- Popular recordings often include a saxophone or trumpet solo in the arrangement.

- Jazz, country, Latin, and gospel bands all have rhythm sections.

Successful arrangers are also researchers who, when necessary, investigate and listen to music styles unfamiliar to them in order to complete projects in a professional and satisfying manner. *Although it does not create a musical style, arranging molds the music within a style.*

While studying arranging technique, it is necessary to write many examples and experiment with different aspects of the technique. It is also essential to have the material performed as often as possible. The strongest insights will result from hearing how different instrumental combinations sound performing arranged passages. Consider these representative questions:

- Should the melody be played by trombone or soprano saxophone? Why?

- Do electric guitar and baritone saxophone sound well in unison, in octaves, or in neither?

- Where in its range does the trumpet begin to overpower the other instruments, and does this change from one situation to another?

- How do various combinations of instruments sound when voicing chords?

Practical experiences in writing arrangements will provide a functional perspective and answers to the many questions that come up. As in other creative pursuits, a high skill level is a product of continued effort and preparation. Patience, professional habits, and a love of the craft of arranging are essential. Quality workmanship will increase the possibilities for performances.

1

JAZZ-BAND INSTRUMENTATION

An arranger's skills are shaped by a combination of artistic maturity and technical proficiency. Artistic maturity develops from repeated exposure to creative music. Technical proficiency, a product of dedicated practice, must include a thorough knowledge of the capabilities and tonal properties of various band instruments.

HISTORICAL OVERVIEW

Jazz and the instrumentation associated with its performance have an interesting history filled with talented and flamboyant personalities. The following information is presented as:

1. an overall perspective

2. an initial source of research and listening possibilities relevant to the craft of arranging.

Rhythm Section

Ragtime and blues performers accompanied themselves on banjo and guitar. Many of these early artists ultimately switched to piano. *Rhythm sections* in the first New Orleans jazz bands usually consisted of both piano and banjo, with tuba and drums. Johnny St. Cyr was the most famous banjoist of the time. Three of the early keyboard masters were Scott Joplin, Jelly Roll Morton, and James P. Johnson. Over the following decades, many outstanding pianists—among them, Art Tatum, Bud Powell, Oscar Peterson, and Bill Evans—ensured that the piano would retain its stature as the preeminent musical instrument.

As early styles progressed and musicians moved north from New Orleans, the double bass eventually replaced the tuba in the rhythm section. In the early 1940s, Jimmy Blanton and Oscar Pettiford, both of whom worked with Duke Ellington, the great composer and pianist, were chiefly responsible for modernizing the function of the bass in creative jazz ensembles. Blanton broke away from the strict two-beat pulse usually assigned to the bass; Pettiford was the first brilliant bass soloist.

During the 1930s, Lionel Hampton, a virtuoso vibraphonist, who achieved fame as a member of the Benny Goodman quartet, brought the vibraphone to prominence in jazz ensembles. Red Norvo and Milt Jackson would emerge in the mid-1940s as the two other important vibraphonists of the time. During the same period, Charlie Christian was exciting his contemporaries with his great jazz solos on electric guitar. Chrisw9an also worked with Goodman, as well as with many of the innovators in the evolving bebop movement. He firmly established the electric guitar in the realm of improvisatory music. Christian's brilliance was such that he was the guitar's standard-bearer for thirty years, until the advent of the rock movement. As the many developments in jazz took place, the role of the drummer was shaped by the influences of Dixieland's Baby Dodds, the swing era's Gene Krupa, and beboppers Kenny Clarke and Max Roach.

Woodwinds

The clarinet was the most popular woodwind instrument played by Dixieland jazz musicians. During the 1920s, when American dance bands were coming into vogue, bandleaders started adding the saxophone to their instrumentation. Previously a novelty instrument, it had a distinctive tonal quality that caught on quickly. The saxophone section soon was the front line in many large ensembles. In addition, the saxophone became the most prominent solo horn in the performance of contemporary music. When Adolphe Sax invented the saxophone in the mid-nineteenth century, he had intended it for use in the performance of "serious" music. However, while art-music composers continue to write for it frequently, the saxophone remains primarily associated with jazz and popular music. Modern players in these fields have more of an "edge" to their sound that sometimes does not sit well with purists. Nevertheless, the saxophone is a dynamic and versatile instrument.

Saxophones come in several sizes; different-sized saxophones have different transpositions. Four models are predominant: soprano, alto, tenor, and baritone. Alto and tenor saxophonists are traditionally the highest profile players, but soprano and baritone have had many famous performers. In the first half of the twentieth century, Sidney Bechet was the most important soprano saxophonist. However, it was Steve Lacy in the mid-1950s, and John Coltrane a few years later, who brought the soprano saxophone to prominence. Many players since then have starred on the instrument. During the bebop era, the electrifying virtuoso Charlie Parker established the alto saxophone as one of the dominant voices in jazz and an exciting solo instrument. Other masters have been Johnny Hodges, Sonny Stitt, and Julian "Cannonball" Adderley. The tenor saxophone is a glamor instrument and is the highest profile solo horn voice in jazz and popular music. Over the years, great performers—including Coleman Hawkins, Lester Young, Sonny Rollins, John Coltrane, and Joe Henderson—elevated the tenor saxophone to its lofty status. Harry Carney, Gerry Mulligan, and Pepper Adams are among the most renowned baritone saxophonists.

In spite of the saxophone, the clarinet has maintained its significant position as an ensemble and soloing instrument. Two clarinet models are common in contemporary music: soprano, simply referred to as clarinet, and bass clarinet. The Dixieland era's top clarinetists were Johnny Dodds, Barney Bigard, and Pee Wee Russell. During the Swing era of the 1930s and 40s, many stars of the clarinet brought the instrument to a level of popularity in the jazz world that has not been equaled since then. Bandleader Benny Goodman was the first true superstar on the clarinet. A superb technician, he was a virtuoso of both jazz and classical music. Other outstanding clarinetists of the time were bandleaders Artie Shaw and Jimmy Dorsey. Later, Jimmy Hamilton, playing clarinet in addition to saxophone, achieved fame in the bands of Duke Ellington. Buddy DeFranco, a master bebop performer on clarinet, and Eddie Daniels— like Goodman, accomplished in jazz and classical music—are two more significant performers.

The flute has taken its place on the jazz scene, sometimes as a player's specialty, often as a double for saxophonists (see DOUBLING on pages 153–56). The flute comes in a number of sizes with different transpositions. The piccolo is the smallest regular member of symphony orchestras and concert bands. The alto and bass flutes are two other models occasionally in use. However, musicians play the soprano-model flute almost exclusively, especially in jazz and popular groups. Eric Dolphy and Hubert Laws are two of the most celebrated jazz flutists. Dolphy, a superb woodwinds player, was also recognized for his virtuosity as a bass clarinetist.

Brasses

Brass instruments were originally featured in street ensembles, small dance bands, and marching bands. The cornet was the principal soprano voice of the brasses. As musicians began expanding their ideas and playing more "hot" music, Joe "King" Oliver emerged as the preeminent cornetist who performed in the evolving jazz idiom. He inspired and supported a brilliant young talent named Louis Armstrong, who went on to achieve immortality. Armstrong's technique and sound were unprecedented, his influence universal. In the mid-1920s, Armstrong switched from cornet to trumpet, apparently because he considered the trumpet sound more rounded and brighter. The trumpet went on to become the jazz band's other principal front-line horn with the saxophone. The list of superstar trumpeters includes Bix Beiderbecke, Roy Eldridge, Dizzy Gillespie, Clifford Brown, and Miles Davis.

The trombone is the other widely played brass instrument in jazz groups. The most prominent Dixieland celebrity on the instrument was Edward "Kid" Ory. The first widely influential trombonist, Jack Teagarden, rose to fame in the 1920s and became the top soloist on his instrument during the swing era. Tommy Dorsey and Glenn Miller, two other accomplished trombonists of the swing era, went on to front popular big bands. Among several outstanding bebop trombonists, J.J. Johnson and Curtis Fuller have been two of the most important. Although the tenor model is predominant among the various trombone models, it is common to include bass trombone in the brass sections of larger ensembles.

The horn and tuba are two other brass instruments that can be used to advantage in jazz arrangements. They appear infrequently in small jazz combos, but are often included by arrangers in larger ensembles. Both can be effective soloing instruments in the hands of capable players. The horn is often called the French horn, although the former is its proper name.

TRANSPOSITION

Instruments not sounding the written pitch they are playing are ***transposing*** instruments, and are classified by the pitch they produce when playing a written C. For instance, a B♭ trumpet playing a written C will sound B♭, one whole step below; but an E♭ alto saxophone playing the same C will sound E♭, a major sixth below. Conversely, ***concert-pitched*** instruments sound the written pitch they are playing and are classified as ***nontransposing***. To sound the identical pitches played by a nontransposing instrument, the B♭ trumpet must produce tones one whole step higher to compensate for the fact that it is pitched one whole step lower than concert pitch. Similarly, the E♭ alto saxophone must produce tones a major sixth higher to compensate for the fact that it is pitched a major sixth lower. A benefit of transposition is that instruments of the same family have virtually identical fingerings and ranges. Example 1–1 outlines transposition.

Each family of instruments has large models with deep voices sounding an octave lower than their smaller counterparts. Those instruments that are not concert-pitched transpose up a major second or sixth plus an octave, instead of just a second or sixth—a critical factor with respect to balance in an arranged passage (Example 1–2).

Example 1–1. *Transposition*

While some uncommon instrument models have other transpositions, jazz band instruments are pitched in one of the keys listed here.

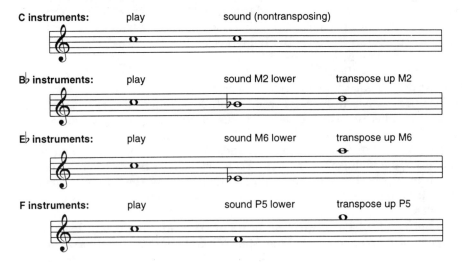

Example 1–2. *Transposition for large-model horns*

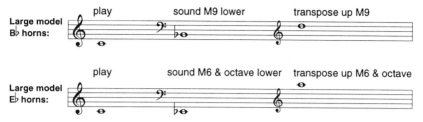

Example 1–3. *Transposing notes and key signatures*

Transposition applies to key signatures also—e.g., if music is in the key of G major, then the key signature is raised a major second to A major for a B♭ instrument and a major sixth to E major for an E♭ instrument. In addition, because wind instruments play in either treble or bass clef, music notated in the bass clef must often be shifted to the treble clef when transposed (see the discussion on SCORE on page 29). The ensuing discussion of individual instruments will specify their proper clefs. (Transposition of chord progressions will be examined in Chapter 2.) Example 1–3 further illustrates transposition.

INSTRUMENT PROPERTIES AND RANGES

- In referring collectively to woodwinds and brasses, musicians often use the term ***horns***—this should not be confused with the instrument named the "horn."

- The saxophone and clarinet are often designated as ***reeds***. This stems from the fact that each instrument uses a mouthpiece that has a cane or plastic reed clamped to it with a device called a *ligature*. A player blows through the mouthpiece, causing the reed to vibrate and generate sound. The flute is also generally understood to be a member of the reeds, although its sound is produced in a different manner; it has an opening in the head joint over which a player blows, similar to blowing across the open end of a bottle.

- All brass instruments have metal cup-shaped mouthpieces. Cup depth and overall mouthpiece size vary, depending on the particular brass instrument and the preferences of individual players. A brass musician produces sound by regulating lip pressure against the mouthpiece and air flow through the instrument.

- The placement and function of a player's lips, mouth, and jaw on the mouthpiece of any wind instrument is termed the *embouchure*.

- Some wind instruments have different models that come with extra keys or attachments that enable them to extend the lower end of the range. Upper ranges of some instruments can also be stretched significantly with special fingerings on the reeds and advanced embouchure technique on the brasses.

- Extreme higher and lower notes in the standard ranges of instruments, especially any of the horns, are usually not practical in harmonized passages or fast playing.

The upcoming discussion of the individual rhythm section and wind instruments includes their specific transpositions and complete standard ranges. The range charts of the instruments should be interpreted as follows:

- **o** The span between whole notes represents the most suitable range of an instrument with respect to arranging procedures.

- **●** The solid notes indicate the extreme higher and lower notes of an instrument's standard range.

- **(●)** Notes enclosed in parenthesis indicate extended lower ranges produced using extra keys or attachments.

Piano

The piano is the most popular instrument in the world. It is concert pitched and has eighty-eight keys encompassing a range of over seven octaves. Depressing a key propels a *hammer* into strings with the resulting vibrations producing a pitch. As long as the key remains depressed, a *damper* is lifted, allowing the note to decay gradually. The strings in the highest octave and a half, with no sustaining strength at all, have no dampers. Depending on where in the range a note is played, the strings being struck will number between one and three and will vary in thickness. When a key is released, the damper falls against the string(s) again and the note dies out immediately. The lower notes are full and very resonant, the middle ones smoother, and the highest notes have a clear, bell-like timbre. Pianos range in size and design. Larger pianos will naturally produce richer sounds and allow for more resonance and definition of sound in the higher and lower ranges. Of the piano's three foot pedals, the most important is the ***damper pedal***, which, when depressed, lifts all dampers. A pianist performs a variety of functions that includes playing chord progressions, specific notated parts, and lead playing. In melodic or solo passages, the player can perform lead lines and chords simultaneously. See Example 1–4.

Electric Guitar

The electric guitar is concert pitched and has a range of almost four octaves. To save space and the excessive use of ledger lines, guitar parts are written an octave higher than actual sound. There are three types of electric guitar: hollow body, semihollow body, and solid body. Because of the huge rock-and-roll movement in the second half of the twentieth century, the electric guitar has had an impact on all contemporary genres of music, including jazz. The instrument, because of its amplification and the multitude of electronic effects available, provides many possible uses to an arranger. A guitarist, modifying the sounds of the instrument to suit the music being performed, provides anything from swinging chord playing to the most obtuse rock sounds. The electric guitar is effective in combination with any of the horns and is also an excellent soloing instrument. See Example 1–5.

Example 1–4. *Piano*

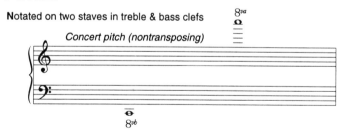

Example 1–5. *Electric guitar*

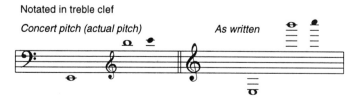

Double Bass

Other names for the double bass are *acoustic bass, upright bass, string bass, contrabass,* or simply *bass*. It is concert pitched and has a range of over three octaves. To save space and the excessive use of ledger lines, bass parts are written an octave higher than actual sound. It is common procedure for players to amplify their instruments. The bass is a very large instrument and presents imposing technical demands on the performer. Talented jazz bassists produce rich, "fat" sounds, performing predominately **pizzicato (pizz.)**—i.e., "plucked" or "fingered." Bowed passages, designated **arco**, are very effective, and arrangers frequently include them in their writing. The bass generally supplies the chordal architecture in arrangements and group improvisation, spelling out the chords as the performance unfolds, and creating the foundation upon which the other band members can weave their lines. Still, creative arrangers have the option of supplying the bass with lead passages or writing specific parts for it within the ensemble. The bass is also a soloing instrument; indeed, talented players are capable of virtuoso ideas even on such a cumbersome instrument. See Example 1–6.

Electric Bass

The electric bass is concert pitched and is notated in the same way as the acoustic bass. Because of its electronics and solid body construction, it has more sustaining possibilities than the acoustic instrument. The bridge that supports the strings on an electric bass is flat. As a result, the strings are equidistant from the neck of the instrument. Therefore, because conventional bowing methods are not possible, electric bassists perform pizzicato. Although the electric bass presents obvious advantages in styles such as rock and fusion, its functions in jazz ensembles are the same as those of the acoustic bass. Electric basses also come in five-string and six-string models that provide wider ranges and tonal possibilities. Range information on the electric bass in this study pertains solely to the four-string model.

Vibraphone

The vibraphone is a percussion instrument with definite pitch. It is nontransposing and has a range of three octaves. The vibraphone is equipped with metal bars that the player strikes with mallets having heads made of yarn or harder, synthetic materials. Talented performers can play with two, three, or

Example 1–6. *Double bass*

four mallets at a time, thus allowing for either single line music, more complex contrapuntal music, or chord playing. As a result of the vibraphone's metal construction, there is good definition to the attack when a note is struck, the sound becoming progressively brighter, the higher one plays in the range. Because the vibraphone itself does not have much sustaining power, the instrument, like the piano, has a damper pedal. When the pedal is depressed, pitches struck will decay gradually. The vibraphone also has **resonators**, tubes located beneath the metal bars that have small paddles attached to shafts. An electric motor allows the paddles to rotate at different speeds and produce various degrees of vibrato. The role of the vibraphone in the jazz ensemble is the same as that of the piano and guitar. See Example 1–7.

Drums

The drummer is the main timekeeper in a jazz ensemble. Drums provide the drive and generate the specific rhythms being performed. The drum kit contains a *snare drum*, *bass drum*, other drums of different timbres, and an array of metal *cymbals* which come in various diameters. Modern drum heads are made of synthetic, resonant plastics. On a snare drum the snares are several strands of wound metal stretched across the bottom drum head, which produce a vibrating "buzzing" sound when the drum head is struck. Snare drums are also equipped with a lever device that will loosen and turn off the snares when desired. The two cymbals always in a drum set are:

1. the larger *ride cymbal*, on which the steady beat of a particular style is performed

2. the smaller *crash cymbal*, which is used primarily for rhythmic accents and punctuation.

Kits vary in the number and the physical dimension of the pieces, based on the tastes and conceptions of individual players. A multitude of sticks, mallets, and other beaters, made with a variety of materials, is available for the drummer's use. Although not required for melodic playing, drummers will tune the various drums in their kits to pitches of their preference. This is accomplished by tightening or loosening a series of bolts, called **lugs**, in the rims holding the drum heads. As a result, the combination of drums and cymbals produces a cohesive sonority. Drum parts are notated on a single standard staff.

Example 1–7. *Vibraphone*

Notated in treble clef

Concert pitch (nontransposing)

Soprano Saxophone

All saxophones are made of brass, each model having its own specific sound. The fingerings and written parts for the instruments are identical and all have a natural range of almost three octaves. The soprano saxophone, a transposing instrument pitched in B♭ that sounds a major second lower than written, is the highest pitched of the commonly played saxophones. In spite of its brass construction, it has somewhat of the lush woodwind sonority in its lower notes. Although it loses this quality and becomes increasingly clearer while ascending through the range, the overall sound of the soprano saxophone is very beautiful. As a rule, both quiet and rapid passages in the bottom end of the range are difficult to execute except by highly skilled players. This is true for all the saxophones, although the lowest notes of the baritone saxophone are somewhat easier to control dynamically. See Example 1–8.

Alto Saxophone

The alto saxophone is a transposing instrument pitched in E♭ that sounds a major sixth lower than written. It possesses a uniformly warm, full sound throughout its range. Although the alto naturally has a deeper voice than the soprano, it is usually the top voice, the *lead alto*, in a saxophone section and often states the melody in a mixed ensemble. The alto saxophone performs well in all styles, from the most tender ballads to up-tempo, soaring passages. See Example 1–9.

Tenor Saxophone

The tenor saxophone is a transposing instrument pitched in B♭ that sounds a major ninth lower than written. It has a deep lower voice capable of being either smooth and rich or strong and gutsy. The sound is robust throughout most of the range with even the highest notes possessing some depth. Like its alto counterpoint, the tenor saxophone functions well in all styles and is very agile. See Example 1–10.

Example 1–8. *Soprano saxophone in B♭*

Written parts notated in treble clef

Example 1–9. *Alto saxophone in E♭*

Written parts notated in treble clef

Baritone Saxophone

The baritone saxophone is a transposing instrument pitched in E♭ that sounds an octave plus a major sixth lower than written. Although the baritone is the biggest saxophone most commonly played, it possesses a wonderful rounded voice and does not have the same penetrating strength in its upper range as the other saxophones. Its bottom notes, in contrast, are very expressive and capable of great definition and intense attack. In addition to the obvious function of being the bottom voice and foundation in a saxophone section, soloists can achieve as much agility with the baritone saxophone as with the other horns. See Example 1–11.

Clarinet

Professional-model clarinets are made of wood and come in several sizes that have different transpositions. The clarinet most widely played is the soprano model, a transposing instrument pitched in B♭. It sounds a major second lower than written and has a natural range of almost four octaves. The clarinet is capable of great agility and breathtaking acrobatics in the hands of an accomplished player. Except for the very highest notes, rapid passages are possible throughout the range. The clarinet sound is appealing and distinctive. In the lower range, known as the ***chalumeau***, the tones are rich and capable of producing very beautiful, fluid passages. In the middle register of the clarinet, the sound loses some of the distinctive "woody" qualities but is nonetheless still full in texture. The upper notes of the clarinet are shriller and more penetrating, yet controllable. See Example 1–12.

Example 1–10. *Tenor saxophone in B♭*

Example 1–11. *Baritone saxophone in E♭*

Example 1–12. *Clarinet in B♭*

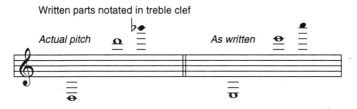

Bass Clarinet

The bass clarinet, a transposing instrument pitched in B♭ that sounds a major ninth lower than written, is the biggest clarinet most commonly played. In spite of its larger size, it is capable of agile passages and possesses many of the same capabilities and an almost identical practical range as the soprano model. Most bass clarinet models have extended lower ranges. The sound of the bass clarinet is full and reedy, especially in the lower notes, which are beautifully resonant. See Example 1–13.

Flute

The flute is nontransposing and has a range of three octaves. Some professional models have an extra key to extend the range a half step lower. The flute is a soprano voice and the highest pitched of the commonly played woodwinds. Like the clarinet, the flute has exceptional agility and is capable of outstanding virtuosity in the hands of a skilled performer. The flute provides wonderful tonal colorings for the arranger. The notes of the lower range are lush and pleasant, but they lack projection and are easily covered among other instruments. Ascending through the range, the flute sound becomes increasingly clear and penetrating. See Example 1–14.

Trumpet

A trumpet has three valves; different pitches are produced by blowing through the instrument and depressing the valves in various combinations. Trumpets come in several sizes with different transpositions. In jazz and popular music the trumpet in use is a transposing instrument pitched in B♭ that sounds a major second lower than written. The trumpet is the soprano voice of the brass section and has a practical range of about two-and-a half octaves. It is an excellent soloing instrument, capable of exciting dexterity in the hands of an accomplished player. In addition to the obvious bravado stylings, the trumpet is also capable of fluid, lush playing. With the exception of the lowest few notes, trumpet sound is rounded and has potential strength throughout the range. The

Example 1–13. *Bass clarinet in B♭*

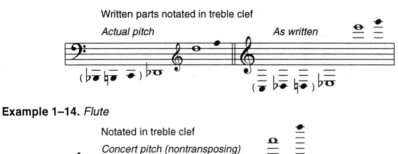

Example 1–14. *Flute*

projection of the trumpet begins to increase significantly above the treble clef. This is important with respect to proper ensemble balance and a player's endurance. A trumpeter who specializes in high notes, called a **lead trumpet player**, possesses a developed embouchure and is capable of extending the upper range significantly. These extreme pitches, often called **screech notes**, are exciting in the performance of lead lines in ensemble passages and as the top notes in chords and percussive passages. Screech notes are very loud and will carry above all other instruments. Used in the proper context, good lead trumpet writing adds zest and definition to an arrangement. See Example 1–15.

Flugelhorn

The flugelhorn, pitched in B♭, has the same transposition and normal range as the trumpet. Because it is a bigger horn than the trumpet and has a wider bore, the flugelhorn has less carrying power. Its tone, nonetheless, is rounded and darker, making it an appealing solo instrument. The distinctive sound of the flugelhorn is also ideal for melodic playing and serves as an effective coloring in ensemble writing. Some flugelhorn models come with four valves, allowing the player to increase the range in the lower end. See Example 1–16.

Trombone

The trombone is a nontransposing instrument, has a normal range of about two and a half octaves, and is the only brass instrument with a slide. In addition to blowing through the horn, a trombonist moves the slide through seven positions. This varies the length of tubing through which the player blows, enabling the production of different pitches. The tenor trombone is the most commonly played model. Although it is a nontransposing horn, it is categorized as a B♭ instrument because the fundamental note produced when the slide is in first position is B♭. The fundamental notes for each slide position are called the **pedal**

Example 1–15. *Trumpet in B♭*

Example 1–16. *Flugelhorn in B♭*

tones. Although all are possible to produce, the first four are the strongest and most practical. The trombone is capable of playing at all dynamic levels and has significant projection and carrying power. An excellent soloing instrument, its agility is better in the upper part of the range because of the increased number of slide positions available for each note. Arrangers must remember that the lower notes have fewer available slide positions. Therefore, careless writing for the lower register of the trombone may require excessive arm movement and may create formidable technical challenges for some players. An example often cited is that of playing from low A♯ to B, a situation requiring a shift from slide position I to VII. A trombonist who specializes in high notes is called a *lead trombone player*. See Example 1–17.

Bass Trombone

The bass trombone has a larger bore and bell than its tenor counterpart and its sound is darker. Like the tenor trombone, it is nontransposing, but it is categorized in a key other than C—in this case, F, its fundamental pitch in first position. The significant feature of the bass trombone is its ability to perform the lowest notes with strength and quality of sound. Although it has similar properties and technically the same range as the tenor model, it seldom plays the very highest notes, except perhaps in soloing situations. The bass trombone is equipped with an *F attachment*, a trigger, operated with the left thumb, that opens extra tubing on the horn. This enables the production of extra notes down a major third to a low C, as well as strong pedal tones from B♭ downward. (Some tenor trombone models also have F attachments.) Some bass trombones have an additional *E attachment*, required to play the low B♮. Other models even have a *D attachment*, further facilitating the production of low notes. The lowest notes are best suited for chords, pedals, or sustained tones. See Example 1–18.

Example 1–17. *Tenor trombone in B♭*

Example 1–18. *Bass trombone in F*

Horn

The horn has three valves and is a transposing instrument pitched in F that sounds a perfect fifth lower than written. Many horn models come equipped with a trigger that, when operated by the left thumb, cuts off tubing and converts the instrument into a B♭ horn. This allows the player to perform the higher notes with more ease. An arranger need only write for an F horn because a player with a double horn will make the performance decisions. The horn has a playable range of almost four octaves. The low end does not project well and is suitable for slower playing or sustained notes. The remainder of the range is flexible. The middle octave and a half, rich and majestic sounding, constitutes the horn's most useful area for melodic playing. It is not possible to play the extreme upper notes quietly and it is best to approach them in a moving line rather than to attack them outright. An arranger must keep the player's stamina in mind and use these highest notes only when desiring dominant horn sound. See Example 1–19.

Tuba

Tubas come in several models and sizes. All have four valves. The two most common tubas, the double C (CC) and double B♭ (BB♭) models, have a range of over three octaves. Because the identifications refer only to fundamental pitches, both models are nontransposing. For such a big horn, the tuba has an overall rounded sound. The midrange notes are best for the performance of melodic material. The low notes are heavy, but they are effective in sustained or slower playing. The high notes, though tending to thin out, are quite penetrating. The tuba, a surprisingly dexterous instrument, requires a large amount of air to be played. An arranger can use the instrument effectively, but should avoid lengthy passages and provide occasional rest for the player. See Example 1–20.

Example 1–19. *Horn in F*

Example 1–20. *Tuba in CC or BB♭*

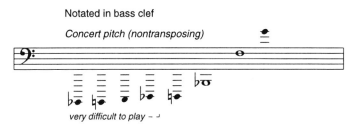

BRASS MUTING

Brass muting decreases the loudness and varies the overall coloring of instruments. It also provides an alternative mode of presentation for soloists. An arranger must indicate in writing on a player's part the manner of muting desired. It is most common to use a *mute*, a cone-shaped device that fits into the bell of an instrument and changes its basic sound, tonal quality, and projection. When a mute is indicated, the player should be given ample time to insert it, a measure or so depending on the tempo of the music. When the mute is no longer required, the arranger writes "open" on the instrument part. Whereas several mutes are available for trumpet and trombone, the cup mute is the standard choice when the two instruments are playing together. Although mutes are made for horn and tuba, they are not often found in use. Of the many methods of brass muting, the following are the most common.

Straight Mute

The *straight mute*, made of fiberboard, plastic, or metal, has the most sound penetration of any mute. It is open at the tapered end and closed at the wide end. The mute is wedged into the instrument bell and held in place by strips of cork on its tapered end. As a result, not all of the sound passes directly through the mute. The straight mute gives the instrument a slightly pinched sound.

Cup Mute

The cone portion of a cup mute is similar to that of the straight mute and is also held in place by strips of cork. Attached to the wide end of the cone is a cup-shaped device. This *cup mute*, made of fiberboard, deadens the sound of the instrument, leaving very little resonance.

Harmon Mute

The *harmon mute* is made of metal. The tapered end is covered completely with cork, causing the sound to pass entirely through the mute. The wide end of the mute has an opening into which a stem can be inserted. The player performs with the stem in or out. With the stem in, the sound is rather raspy. Without the stem, the sound is very neutral and without resonance—the famous sound of the great Miles Davis.

Plunger

The *plunger* is identical with the end of the toilet tool of the same name. When it is held close to the bell, the instrument produces a less distinct sound. When the plunger is held against the bell during rapid or articulated playing, a cracking sound can be produced. The plunger is often used to perform a bluesy "wa-wa" effect by alternately covering and uncovering the bell. This is notated with + over a note to designate "covered" and o to designate "uncovered."

Into the Stand

"Into the stand" is assigned predominantly to brass instruments. It instructs a player to blow directly into the stand with the instrument bell a few inches from it. This reduces the volume of the instrument while maintaining a good quality of sound and allowing for normal playing. The procedure often produces effective results for passages written in the upper ranges of brass instruments, ensuring robust sound that is not overbearing.

Summary

Trumpet:	Straight Mute
	Cup Mute
	Harmon Mute
	Plunger
	Into the stand
Trombone:	Cup Mute
	Plunger
	Into the stand
Horn, Tuba:	Straight Mute

EXERCISES

1. Review the information on the characteristics and tonal properties of jazz-band instruments. Commit to memory:
   a. which instruments are nontransposing (concert pitched);
   b. which instruments are transposing. For these instruments, what are their specific transpositions.

2. Review the information on brass muting.

3. Review all relevant notational procedures.

4. Review fundamental harmonic practice.

5. Listen regularly to recordings of jazz and other contemporary styles of music—primarily instrumental performances. Listen to ensembles of all sizes. Become familiar with the particular sonorities of the individual instruments.

6. Attend as many live jazz concerts as possible.

7. Rewrite the following passages transposed for the indicated instruments. Remember that the key signatures should also be transposed.

2

PREPARATORY INFORMATION

TERMINOLOGY

Contemporary music has an operating langauage that combines traditional terms with its own indigenous expressions. The following terminology is used regularly by arrangers, composers, and instrumentalists.

Head

Jazz musicians use the term *"head"* to designate the original melody of a composition or arrangement.

Straight Ahead

Contemporary musicians have adopted the term *"straight ahead"* to denote when music is to be considered or performed in an ordinary manner—in other words, the music, whatever style it is, should not be too jazzed up or overly arranged.

Chart

Contemporary musicians often refer to arrangements as ***charts***. In this respect, a printed copy of an arrangement may also be called a chart. (See the discussion on SCORE on page 29.)

Soli

Soli is the term used to designate a passage in which the instruments of one section within an ensemble perform together. The particular make-up of a band will often determine what constitutes a soli. For example, in a large band comprised of several trumpets, trombones, and saxophones, each section would be obviously discernible. On the other hand, in a small band with only one trumpet, trombone, and saxophone, or any small combination of instruments, a soli would probably consist of a mixed group of instruments.

Tutti

Tutti is the term used to designate a passage in which all the sections of an ensemble perform together, either in identical or various rhythms.

Consonance/Dissonance

Consonance refers to smooth, mellow sound produced by two or more notes played simultaneously. Popular and easy-listening music, or any other non-adventurous styles, are predominantly consonant. In general, consonant music will appeal to the traditionally oriented or "average" listener, who has never studied music formally or been exposed to more sophisticated styles. This does not mean that consonant music is not embraced by and useful to creative artists. Consonance can certainly be employed in original and moving ways depending on musical context and an arranger's resourcefulness.

Dissonance is the antithesis of consonance. It refers to a more biting sound—something that may grate on one's senses. For example, the murder scene in a movie, such as the shower scene in *Psycho*, could have foreboding background music that contains dissonance. Widespread commercial potential in music tends to decrease as dissonance increases. Unfortunately, the avant-garde is often negatively associated with dissonance. In any case, it is possible for dissonant music to be positive, beautiful, and even commercially viable. An accomplished arranger will use dissonance to advantage and place it in its proper context.

The terms consonance and dissonance are useful in that their general meanings are understood universally. The actual consonance and dissonance found in music passages or configurations may not, however, be similarly perceived by different musicians or musicians in different cultures. An individual's training, orientation, and experiences will be significant factors in determining how he or she hears and treats music.

NOTATIONAL PROCEDURE

An arranger's work must be clearly organized. Accurate music notation is essential. In a study environment a reasonable number of inaccuracies or immature decisions are acceptable. However, *needless* errors are a problem. Messy work or carelessly notated music inevitably hinders rehearsals and performances in both study and professional situations. When writing by hand, it is always a good idea to use pencil and to make high-quality photocopies of final drafts. When using computer software, all work should be proofread as carefully as if it had been handwritten. Following is a review of the notational procedures used most often in arranging work.

Tempo

Tempo is the speed or rate of forward motion of a musical work. It is often indicated by a ***metronome marking*** at the beginning or at any point in the work where the arranger wishes a new tempo to occur. A ***metronome*** is a mechanical device, electronic or spring-wound, that can be set to click at different rates of speed. For example, a marking of (q = 120) would signify music at a tempo of 120 beats per minute. It is standard practice for jazz composers and arrangers to include a direction such as "up" or "medium," either with or without a metronome marking, when indicating the desired tempo. Certain terms exist that specify alterations of tempo. Although Italian, French, and German are the three primary non-English languages of music, the Italian tempo indications are used almost exclusively. The two most common terms are ***accelerando (accel.)***, meaning "getting faster," and ***ritardando (rit.)***, meaning "slowing down." Tempo markings are placed above the music. Example 2–1 shows how tempo markings are indicated.

Articulation and Phrasing

Articulation and phrasing pertain to the manner of performing music. Though the two terms are sometimes used interchangeably, ***articulation*** essentially concerns individual notes, whereas ***phrasing*** relates to the interpretation of music. Because of the constantly increasing sophistication and complexity in

Example 2–1. *Tempo markings*

composition and music notation, there exists a multitude of phrase and articulation markings that composers and arrangers can use to indicate their intentions in a musical work. Although all notational devices are available, relatively few markings will suffice for a majority of arranging work. Example 2–2 illustrates the most common markings.

Example 2–2. *Common articulation and phrase markings*

1 A dot signifies **staccato**, meaning the note is attacked in a detached manner. The result is that the note duration is shortened, being held for less than its full value. Staccato dots are placed on the note-head side, within or outside the staff.

2 This mark designates an accented note. It is placed outside the staff on the note-head side.

3 This marking designates a strong accent. It is placed outside the staff on the note-head side.

4 Any articulation marking on a whole note is placed as if the note had a stem.

5 A line indicates **tenuto**, meaning "held" or "sustained." No separation should be perceived between notes. A tenuto marking is placed on the note-head side, within or outside the staff.

6 Brief tenuto.

7 Accented tenuto.

8 Slurs and ties are placed on the note-head side.

9 A slur can enclose a tie.

10 When note stems are in both directions, the slur is placed above the notes.

11 If a note repeats under a slur, a line can be placed above the repeated note, indicating a slight attack, so that the second note is discernible.

12 Slurs and on whole notes should be placed as if the notes had stems.

Glissando, Fall-off, Doit

Running or sliding through consecutive notes to a target note is called a *glissando*. Musicians often shorten the term to *gliss*. A gliss is indicated with a diagonal line and is performed with either a definite or indefinite beginning pitch (Example 2–3a). "Gliss" may be written above the diagonal line as well as "long" or "short" to ensure that a player understands the arranger's intention. String players can actually slide up a string to produce a gliss. Horn players, with the exception of trombonists, finger the run of notes, although the pitches need not be distinct. In many cases trombonists can produce a true gliss by sliding up the series of pitches. A *fall-off* is the opposite of a gliss in that it occurs at the end of a phrase or passage and the player runs downward from the beginning pitch (Example 2–3b). A *doit* is performed primarily by the brasses; the player produces an upward gliss at the end of a phrase or passage (Example 2–3b).

Fermata

The *fermata* (⌢) is a hold or pause. It indicates that a note is to be held longer than its actual duration and cut off on cue (Example 2–4). The fermata sign is usually placed above a note. In some cases, in order to save space, or when there is more than one part on a staff, the fermata may be placed below the note. Although fermatas are frequently used at the end of an arrangement, they may be applied at any point during the work.

Example 2–3. *Glissando, Fall-off, Doit*

Example 2–4. *Fermata*

Dynamics

Dynamics is the term that pertains to volume or degrees in loudness of music. Letter abbreviations of Italian words—e.g., *p*, *mf*, *sfz*, etc.— signify relative volumes at which music is performed. Two Italian terms are used to indicate alterations in loudness. They are *crescendo (cresc.)*, meaning "becoming louder," and *decrescendo (decresc.)*, meaning "becoming quieter." These two terms can also be illustrated graphically. Dynamic markings are placed under the music. Example 2–5 illustrates and explains the dynamic marks used most often.

Example 2–5. *Common dynamic markings*

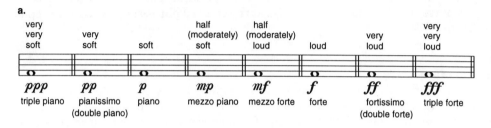

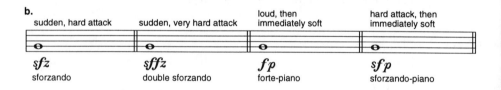

Score

A *score* is the printed version of every aspect of a musical composition or arrangement. It lists all instruments used along with the music they play in the piece, including articulation and phrase markings, dynamics, meter and tempo indications, soloing passages, and anything else the composer/arranger wishes. Scores are utilized by conductors, players, producers, studio technicians, educators, students, other arrangers, and anyone else who wishes to understand and interpret a particular musical work. An arranger has the choice of writing concert-pitched or transposed scores. A concert-pitched score will show all instruments written as they sound. A transposed score shows the transposing instruments at their transposed pitches. Arrangers must acquire facility at working with both types of scores. Whereas *most jazz arrangements have transposed scores*, concert-pitched scores may be more practical for studying and understanding complex works. In any event the arranger decides which type of score to use. To ensure maximum efficiency, there cannot be any confusion with respect to an instrument's proper transposition. (Refer to Appendix 1 for detailed illustrations of scores.)

System

Two or more staves grouped as a unit are called a *system*; thus, all the staves in a score form a system. Families of instruments or instruments comprising an important section of an ensemble are in turn grouped together within the system. Each section is indicated by a thick line, bracket, or brace at its left side on each page of a score. Additionally, bar lines are drawn through the staves of these sections. See Example 2–6. (Refer to Appendix 1 for detailed illustrations of scores.)

Example 2–6. *System and sections*

Parts

A *part* is the printed version of the music performed by an individual instrument. When a score has been completed, the instrumental parts must be extracted (copied out)—and transposed when necessary (as discussed in Chapter 1)—so that the performance can take place. The part will also include everything in the score pertaining to it: meter, tempo, dynamics, articulations, solos, etc. (Example 2–7a). When a transposing instrument is given a solo, the chord progression for its solo must also be transposed accordingly (Example 2–7b). Utmost care must be taken to ensure that an instrument is notated in its proper clef and transposed accurately. (Refer to Appendix 1 for detailed illustrations of parts.)

Example 2–7. *Parts*

a. Articulations, phrasing, and dynamic markings are exactly the same on the parts as on the score.

Score

Transposed up M6

Transposed up M9

b. Chord progressions for soloists must also be transposed when necessary.

Score

E–7   A7   / D Maj7   D7(♭9)   / G–7   C7   / F Maj7   /

Transposed up M2

F♯–7   B7   / E Maj7   E7(♭9)   / A–7   D7   / G Maj7   /

Transposed up M6

C♯–7   F♯7   / B Maj7   B7(♭9)   / E–7   A7   / D Maj7   /

PRINCIPLES OF THEORY

As a convenience, some essential theory information is discussed here. The information is presented as a review and to establish how it is applied to the craft of arranging.

Diatonic Scale

All the major and minor scales, constructed of five whole steps and two half steps, are classified as *diatonic scales*. Melodies, chords, chord progressions, and intervals that are comprised of notes from a particular major or minor scale are diatonic to that scale. Notes belonging to a diatonic scale are called *diatonic notes*.

Chromatic Scale

Notes that do not belong to a diatonic scale are classified as *chromatic*. A chromatic note is indicated with an *accidental*—either a sharp, flat, or natural. The *chromatic scale* is constructed of twelve successive half steps; sharps are used in ascending the scale and flats in descending. The term *chromaticism* refers to the presence or use of chromatic notes, intervals, and chords. A *chromatic chord* contains at least one nondiatonic note.

Interval

An *interval* is the distance between two notes and is designated by a numeral, according to the number of scale degrees it encompasses. For instance, the interval between C and F (C, D, E, F) is called a fourth. A *unison* is an interval consisting of the same note performed simultaneously by two or more instruments. An *octave* is an interval of eight notes. Notes that are an octave apart have the same name; for instance, major and minor scales begin and end with the same note an octave apart. In the major scale, the intervals of the *unison, fourth, fifth*, and *octave* are called *perfect*. Intervals of the *second, third, sixth*, and *seventh* are called *major*. When a major interval is lowered by a half step, it becomes a *minor* interval. When a perfect interval is lowered by a half step, it becomes a *diminished* interval. When either a major or a perfect interval is raised by a half step, it becomes an *augmented* interval. There are numerous possible alterations and several of the resulting intervals are useful only in theory. See Example 2–8 for the list of intervals that are most pertinent in arranging.

Example 2–8. *Intervals used in arranging*

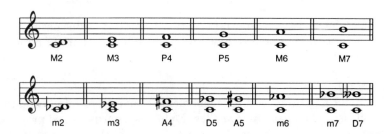

A *simple* interval is an interval of an octave or less. A *compound* interval, which consists of more than an octave, can be thought of as a simple interval whose span is increased by an octave. For instance, a ninth is an interval of a second plus an octave (Example 2–9).

The *inversion* of an interval occurs when the order of the two notes is switched—i.e., the bottom note is shifted to become the top one. Seconds and sevenths, thirds and sixths, and fourths and fifths are inversions of each other. The different intervals produce their own particular degrees of consonance and dissonance. In arranging, the intervallic relationship of musical elements, such as chord voicings (see VOICING on pages 33–35) or line against line, is extremely important because it will have a lot to do with the resultant mood and emotional impact of the music. For arranging purposes interval classification applies as follows:

1. *Unisons/octaves* and all major and minor thirds and sixths are consonant intervals. *Major thirds/minor sixths* and *major sixths/minor thirds* are inversions of each other. They are also the most consonant intervals.

2. *Perfect fourths/perfect fifths* are inversions of each other and are the next level of consonance—more open and pure in sound.

3. *Major seconds/minor sevenths* are inversions of each other and are somewhat dissonant.

4. *Minor seconds/major sevenths* are inversions of each other and are the most dissonant intervals.

Example 2–9. *Compound intervals used in arranging*

Example 2–10 illustrates these intervals together with their inversions grouped and ordered with respect to their particular levels of consonance and dissonance.

Tritone

A *tritone* is the only interval that, when inverted, remains exactly the same interval. This is because the tritone divides the octave in half. The distance covered by a tritone is three whole tones, hence its name. The tritone is the most unstable interval; a chord containing a tritone will want to move in a progression. Dominant and diminished chords, which are so important in cadential and modulatory passages, contain a tritone within their structures (Example 2–11).

Voicing

Voicing refers to the particular configuration of notes in a chord. The note on which a chord is based is called its *root*; for instance, the root of a C7 chord is C. A chord has a *closed voicing* when the distance between the two outer notes is an octave or less. A chord voicing is in *root position* when the root is on the bottom and the third, fifth, and (if it is some type of sixth or seventh chord) the sixth or seventh are stacked in ascending order on top. A *first inversion* occurs when the root in a root-position chord is shifted from the bottom of the voicing to the top. Now the third is on the bottom of the voicing. When the third in a first-inversion chord is shifted from the bottom to the top, a *second inversion* results, with the fifth now on the bottom. In a chord with a sixth or seventh, a *third inversion* results when the fifth in a second inversion is shifted to the top of the voicing. In Example 2–12, chords are diagrammed in root position and inversions.

Example 2–10. *Intervals and their inversions*

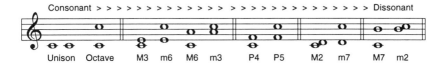

Example 2–11. *The tritone*

Example 2–12. *Chords in root position and inversions*

The intervals between the notes vary from one chord type to another and from inversion to inversion. This is especially significant to arrangers because of the differing impacts and sounds of chords in their various configurations. Chords in root position have notes in specific orderings of major and minor thirds piled up on top of each other. There are two exceptions:

1. An augmented seventh chord has one interval of a major second between the augmented fifth and the flatted seventh.

2. In a sixth chord, major or minor, the sixth is a major second above the fifth.

When chords are inverted, the succession of intervals is altered. Now, any relationships between degrees of the chords, such as root and fifth, third and seventh, etc., are different; we hear the same chord, but with another quality of sound. *The chord name does not change in inversion.*

The augmented triad and the diminished seventh chord are the two chord types whose structures remain consistent when they are inverted; this is because they are both equally spaced chords (Example 2–13).

Extensions

Extensions are so named because they are labeled according to their distance above the seventh in chords. Since chords in root position are constructed in a series of thirds on top of each other, the extensions after the seventh are the ninth, eleventh, and thirteenth (Example 2–14). Extensions are diatonic when they relate directly to the scale from which a chord is built. They are considered chromatic alterations when they do not come from the related scale.

Example 2–13. *Chord types with invariant spacing regardless of inversion*

Augmented triads have consistent spacing of a major third between notes. Inversions will have identical spacing.

Diminished seventh chords have consistent spacing of a minor third between notes. Inversions will have identical spacing.

Example 2–14. *Ninth, eleventh, thirteenth*

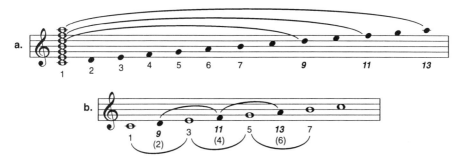

Example 2–15. *Guide tones*

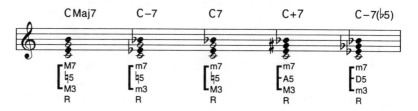

Guide Tones

The specific defining notes of any chord—those notes that determine a chord's quality—are called the *guide tones*. The third and seventh of a chord are always guide tones because they differ from one chord type to another. In both the minor 7(♭5) and the augmented seventh chords, the fifth, because it is altered, is also a guide tone. There are no specific guide tones in a diminished chord because its notes are equidistant from each other (Example 2–15).

EXERCISES

1. Review contemporary music terminology.

2. Notate the specified interval above each note.

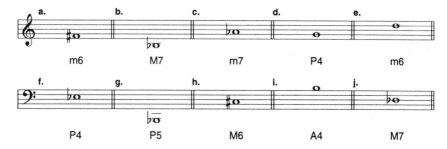

3. Notate the specified chords in close position above each note. Identify the inversions.

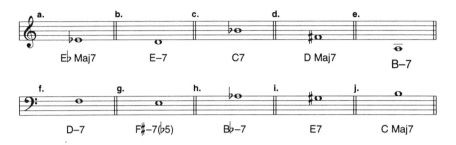

Eb Maj7   E–7   C7   D Maj7   B–7

D–7   F#–7(b5)   Bb–7   E7   C Maj7

4. Identify the complete letter name and inversion of each chord.

5. Transpose the following progressions as indicated.

Up M2

a. E–7(b5)   A7(b9)   / D–7   G7   / C–7   F7   / Bb Maj7   /

Up M6

b. F7   Bb7   / Eb7   Ab7   / Db7   G7   / G Maj7

Up P5

c. C#–7   F#7   / B Maj7   D7   / G Maj7   Bb7   / Eb Maj7   /

Up M6

d. A–7   Ab7   / G–7   Gb7   / F Maj7   F#7   / B Maj7   /

6. Add the indicated extensions as close as possible above the following chords. Identify the guide tones in each chord.

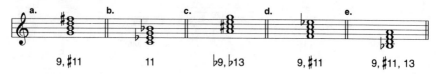

7. Rewrite the following passages transposed as indicated. On each transposed part include all articulations, dynamics, phrase markings, and tempo indications.

3

FORM AND DESIGN

GENERAL INFORMATION

Standards
The majority of popular songs that jazz musicians adapt for performance comes from musical theater. These songs, termed **standards**, constitute the basic repertoire of jazz and popular artists. Conversely, except for the works of Duke Ellington, the music of important jazz composers in the second half of the twentieth century has rarely become part of the popular standard repertoire. Jazz is essentially sophisticated instrumental music without lyrics. As a result, most **jazz standards** are recognized and appreciated primarily by other jazz musicians and devotees.

Verse and Chorus
In its original design, a popular standard is almost always comprised of a verse and chorus. The **verse** is the opening or introductory material and the **chorus**, the main body or message of the song. Jazz musicians rarely include the verse in performance. Instead, they state the chorus and improvise on its chord progression. In fact, many jazz improvisers, unless they are also musical theater buffs, do not even know the verses of standards. Jazz arrangers, like players, also ignore the verses in songs. When there are no restrictions on an arranging project, it is more exciting to create new material, such as introductions, interludes, transitional passages, and original endings (see ADDED COMPONENTS on page 49).

Lead Sheet
A **lead sheet** is the printed copy of a piece of music that shows its title, melody, lyrics (if any), chord progression, and composer(s). Occasionally, information that is vital for the proper realization of the music (e.g., specific bass line, counterline, etc.) will be included on the lead sheet. Lead sheets are used widely by jazz and popular players both as an aid for practicing and as a reference in spontaneous jam sessions or rehearsal situations. When an arranger is

planning to write an arrangement of a standard composition, a lead sheet will contain the basic musical information that is needed to plan the work. It is common practice, wherever possible, to notate jazz lead sheets with four measures per line. A collection of lead sheets in a bound volume, often by genre of music (jazz, Broadway, country, etc.), is called a *fake book*. In this chapter, examples of *form* will be displayed as lead sheets.

COMMON 32-MEASURE FORMS

Form refers to the architecture or structure of a musical work. In standards, verses are generally free in structure while choruses tend to be organized. Consequently, the most common forms in jazz and popular music are those found in the choruses of standards. The number of measures in these standard choruses frequently totals some multiple of 8. Often there are 32 measures, comprised of four 8-measure segments.

AABA
The workhorse of contemporary music is the AABA form. As the letters signify, there are three identical or very similar sections and a fourth section that contains different material. The B section, called the *bridge*, functions as contrasting material to the A sections. (The bridge is sometimes called the *release* although this term is not used much anymore.) Whereas the first two A sections are basically identical, minimal chord or melodic alterations are sometimes necessary in the last measure or two of the second A section to enable a logical transition to the bridge. The end of the final A section may also be slightly altered since it closes the chorus. Example 3–1 illustrates a lead sheet of a 32-measure AABA chorus.

AABC, ABAC
Two other common forms are AABC and ABAC. In AABC, the C section is either altogether different from the A section or dissimilar enough so that it can be considered a new section. In ABAC, both the B and C sections are composed as contasting passages to the A sections. See Example 3–2 (page 42) and Example 3–3 (page 43).

ABCD
Although it is not an unusual form, ABCD does not occur as often as the preceding ones. As the letters indicate, it is the only form wherein each of the four sections contains contrasting material. See Example 3–4 (page 44).

Example 3–1. *32-measure AABA form*

All 32-measure lead-sheet examples in this chapter have their sections marked with bold letters for illustrative purposes only. It is not conventional notation practice to mark lead sheets in this manner— double bar lines at the end of a section will suffice.

Potential

Norman David

Example 3–2. *32-measure AABC form*

E-Flat Mail

Norman David

© 1997 Norman David

Example 3–3. *32-measure ABAC form*

This lead sheet contains first and second endings. See REPEATS AND ENDINGS on pages 46–48 for a detailed description of the use and proper notation of repeats and endings.

Referential

Norman David

Medium Latin

Example 3–4. *32-measure ABCD form*

Conscientious

Norman David

© 1978 Norman David

OPTIONAL FORMS

In addition to these common forms, countless other chorus structures are possible. Composers can design music in any ways their imaginations lead them. Following is a general summary:

1. Choruses are shorter than 32 measures—16-measure and 24-measure choruses are the most common.

2. Choruses are longer than 32 measures, constructed in various combinations of 8-measure and/or 16-measure sections.

3. Choruses are of varying lengths:

    a. combinations of 8-measure sections and irregular-length sections

    b. combinations of 16-measure sections and irregular-length sections

    c. combinations of 8-measure, 16-measure, and irregular-length sections

    d. all irregular-length sections.

Two sample choruses, of lengths other than 32 measures, are shown in Examples 3–5 and 3–6.

Example 3–5. *A 9-measure chorus*

A Memory

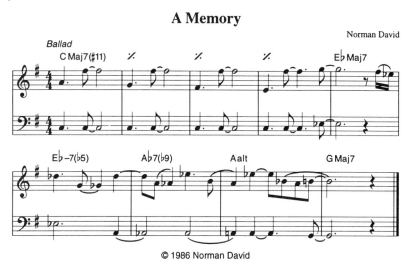

Example 3–6. *A 28-measure (8-8-12) chorus*

Give Me the Ball

Norman David

© 1990 Norman David

REPEATS AND ENDINGS

Repeats are a methods of indicating repeating passages of music, or just a repeated measure or two, to save space and time. Various procedures are outlined in Example 3–7. (See also Examples 3–3, 3–8, and 5–19 (page 75).)

Example 3–7. *Repeated passages and measures*

a. The double barline with the two dots at the end of the passage is a repeat bar. It indicates that all previous eight measures must be repeated. No repeat bar is required at the beginning of a piece of music.

b. Repeat the four measures *between* the repeat bars.

c. Play through the first ending (bracketed with enclosed number 1), go back to the beginning and play through the second ending—*skipping the first ending*—and continue on.

d. A diagonal slash surrounded by two dots indicates that the preceding measure is repeated. In this passage, the music in the first measure would be played three more times.

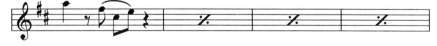

e. Parallel diagonal slashes surrounded by two dots with the number 2 above indicates that the two preceding measures are repeated.

Endings are a means of avoiding the repetition of passages of music that are identical save for the last measure or two in each passage. The lead sheet presented in Example 3–1 is shown again in Example 3–8, this time with first and second endings. With these repeat endings, it is not necessary to renotate the complete first eight measures. The streamlined lead sheet remains easy to read while taking up less space. In any event, arrangers should use repeats and endings only when it appears logical to do so—i.e., when the facility of reading and interpreting the music will not be compromised.

Example 3–8. *A lead sheet with first and second endings*

© 1980 Norman David

ADDED COMPONENTS

Introduction

An *introduction* (*intro*) is opening material before the main body of music. In a sense, the verse of any song is a form of introduction. Although an intro can take many shapes, it must retain its subordinate character and be recognizable for what it is. The design possibilities can be classified as follows:

1. a simple passage of a few chords or short motives

2. a passage containing fragments or hints of melodies to come

3. contrasting material—motivic, melodic, chordal, or any combination.

Coda

A *coda* is a section of music that completes or extends a lead sheet, arrangement, or any presentation of music by introducing new material. The coda can be a brief ending, a new way in which to treat another chorus of the music, a passage that takes an arrangement in another direction, an elaborate closing idea, or any event of varying length and design.

D.C./D.S.

D.C. and D.S. are directional indications. ***D.C.*** *(da capo)* means "from the beginning"; a performer, on seeing this in a part, returns to the beginning of the music and plays to the end. If the direction is ***D.C. al Fine***, the performer plays from the beginning and ends at the indication of ***Fine*** on the part. ***D.S.*** *(dal segno)* means "to the sign," directing the player to go back in the music to where the sign (𝄋) appears and play to the end. If the direction is ***D.S. al Fine***, the performer plays from the sign and likewise ends at Fine. If the direction is either ***D.C. al Coda*** or ***D.S. al Coda***, the player returns to the beginning or the sign and plays to where the coda sign (⊕) appears. At that point, the music skips immediately to the end of the part and continues in a section designated with the coda sign. In Example 3–9, all of these situations are exhibited.

Example 3–9. *D.C. and D.S. indications*

a. Go back to the beginning (D.C.) and play through again.

D.C.

b. **D.C. al Fine:** Back to the beginning and play through until Fine;
D.S. al Fine: Back to the sign and play through until Fine.

Fine

D.C. al Fine

or D.S. al Fine

c. **D.C. al Coda:** Return to the beginning of the part and play to the (⊕) sign. At that point, skip to the music in the coda section at the end of the part.

D.S. al Coda: Return to the (𝄋) sign and play to the (⊕) symbol. At that point, skip to the coda section.

D.C. al Coda

or D.S. al Coda

Tag Ending

A *tag ending*, similar to a coda passage, prolongs the closing of an arrangement. The principle difference is that the tag ending is exactly what it implies: an ending only. It can be a repeated rhythmic figure, a repeated motivic fragment from the melody, or prolonged repetition of the final chord(s) in a piece.

EXERCISES

1. Purchase or borrow fake books and lead sheets. Examine the manner in which publishers and composers notate the music—look for endings, repeats, chord symbols, etc. Analyze the forms of choruses in different songs and compositions. Determine also if there are verses, intros, extended endings, etc.

2. When listening to recordings of standards, analyze their forms before obtaining the printed copies of the music.

3. Rewrite the following lead sheet with first and second endings. Use *D.C. al Coda* instead of the third A section.

© 1997 Norman David

4

MELODY

MELODY/LEAD LINE

A *lead line* is the principal melody and voice in a passage of music. The original melody of a particular composition is, therefore, the defining lead line of that composition. In addition to the original melody, arrangements also contain varying numbers of secondary melodies. These melodies might be the leads in soli passages, background lines, counterlines, or any of the other parts of an arrangement.

The manner in which an arranger works with melodies is crucial to the eventual impact and success of an arrangement. In this respect, arrangers can choose to make alterations to the original melody of a composition. It is frequently more interesting musically to redesign a melody before harmonizing it or adding contrapuntal material. An arranger decides what to do after studying the original lead sheet or sketch, considering the style and tempo of the music, and determining what the instrumentation will be. The present discussion will concern the shaping of melodies—how an arranger might change the melodic rhythm and contour to suit his or her artistic impulses and the musical context of an arrangement. Subsequent chapters will focus on methods of harmonizing lead lines.

Modification

In a $\frac{4}{4}$ measure, the beat most naturally stressed is the first one. Beat 3 is the second most stressed. In a $\frac{3}{4}$ measure, the strongest beat is also the first one. Music notated in these time signatures flows within the framework of the natural stresses. Example 4–1 shows a segment of a melody as it might appear on a lead sheet and three possible modifications of the melody. The original melodic fragment is rhythmically simple and performable at various tempos. By singing the line or just humming the rhythm, the foundational strength of beats 1 and 3 should be apparent. Each melodic alteration has a similar contour and the same notes as the original. The melody has been given a new personality in each case, yet it remains easily recognizable.

The melodic fragment in Example 4–2 is modified twice. In a short phrase, the slightest alterations can change the character of the melody.

Example 4–1. *A melody and three possible modifications*

Example 4–2. *Changing the character of a melody*

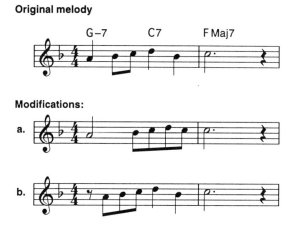

Syncopated Rhythm/Swing

The melodies shown in Examples 4–1 and 4–2 were rhythmically conservative and the important melody notes fell exactly on the beat. Occasionally, an arranger might opt for this straightforward treatment. However, jazz and other creative styles of music flow with melodies and rhythms that often place important attacks and accents off the beat. This definitive rhythmic feature is called *syncopation*. In jazz, melodies with syncopated lines and rhythms are common and integral to the classic *swing* style.

When creating syncopated lines, an arranger must keep the amount of anticipation to one half beat or less in order to generate a swing feel. Adding syncopation to a melody involves a give-and-take process. When a note is anticipated, the length of the anticipation is deducted from the preceding note. In this manner an individual measure retains its proper number of beats. If a melodic note is anticipated by more than one-half beat in advance, an interesting rhythmic effect may result, although the offbeat swing feel has been avoided at that point. Example 4–3 shows two possible variations of the melody of Example 4–1, both containing syncopated rhythms in addition to other notational changes. Some melody notes are now attacked one-half beat earlier; this creates the feeling of swing. In both melodies the flow still centers around beats 1 and 3, while the line remains recognizable and swings. Syncopation in general, and swing specifically, eliminate the "squareness" in music. As a result the music has a basic feeling of pushing forward—driving, yet relaxed, energy at any tempo.

An anticipated attack, whether tied over to the following note or not, feels and functions as if it is part of the action on the following beat. In Example 4–4, the melodic modifications shown in Example 4–3 are given further notational changes. In five instances, marked with asterisks, anticipating attacks are no

Example 4–3. *Swing (syncopated) variations of the melody of Example 4–1*

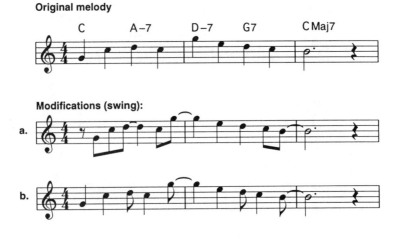

longer tied over to notes on the following beats. Instead, they are followed by rests. The rhythmic effect is identical despite shorter note durations. The forward moving sense of swing remains.

It is possible to modify any melody in some way. In Example 4–5, syncopated rhythm is added to almost every note from an original melodic fragment. This may or may not be overdone. An effective lead line should be balanced as well as rhythmically interesting. If it appears that the music can be altered in an interesting way, then an arranger has the option of modifying that music. Conversely, if a melody is suitable as originally notated or if it needs only minimal changes, it should be treated carefully or simply remain free of alterations. The rhythm and contour of a melody should be appropriate to the musical context. What are the style, tempo, and mood of the music? How is the remainder of the melody going to be phrased? What is the instrumentation at any particular point in the arrangement? How is the melody going to be treated if it occurs again in the arrangement?

Example 4–4. *Anticipating attacks followed by a rest*

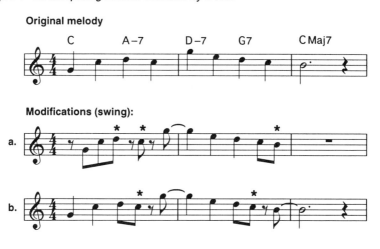

Example 4–5. *Overmodifying a melody.*

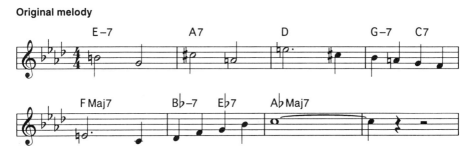

Modifications (swing): *Is this passage overmodified?*

Example 4–6 shows how music in $\frac{3}{4}$ time can swing with the addition of syncopation. In the modified passage, some notes are anticipated on the upbeats from previous measures. In the fourth and fifth measures, the anticipated melodic rhythm results in two dotted quarter notes, dividing the three-beat measure exactly in half. This is one of the defining rhythmic patterns of passages that swing in $\frac{3}{4}$.

Example 4–6. *Adding syncopation in $\frac{3}{4}$*

MELODIC ANALYSIS

To work efficiently with melodies, an arranger must analyze them first, in order to determine how individual melody notes relate to chord progressions and phrasing.

Chord Tones and Extensions

In tonal music the notes in a melody relate in some way to the harmony that supports them. In the most basic melodies, individual notes are simply chord tones (1, 3, 5, 7) or extensions (9, 11, 13). The melodies in Example 4–7 consist solely of tones belonging to the underlying chords.

Passing Tones

A *passing tone* has a duration of a quarter note or less and moves *stepwise* (half or whole) from one important melody note to another. In the majority of cases a passing tone occurs on a nonstressed note in a melodic line. It is important to remember that a note functions as a passing tone in relation to the *movement* of a melody. Consequently, a passing tone can still be a chord tone or extension from the harmony supporting it. In Example 4–8, the first three notes of the melodic fragment can function only as strong melody notes. The remainder of the melody contains three passing tones.

Example 4–7. *Melodies consisting of tones of the underlying chords*

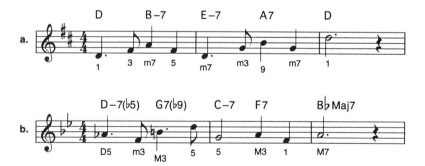

Example 4–8. *Passing tones*

Approach Notes

An *approach note* is similar to a passing tone in that it approaches an important melody note by step (half or whole). The difference is that an approach note does not have to leave a melody note by step—*approach notes need not be prepared*. An approach note is analyzed in relation to its target note.

Scale Approach

A *scale approach note* relates diatonically to the chord supporting its target note. Therefore, scale approaches work best with diatonic chord progressions and often, but not always, with diatonic melodies. The melody of Example 4–9 contains four scale approach notes.

Chromatic Approach

A *chromatic approach note* always moves by half step. Because approach notes are one-half beat or less in duration, a chromatic approach will not be jarring to the ear if it is not part of the underlying harmony. Instead, a chromatic approach note moves naturally to its target note, the half-step motion allowing a smooth resolution to a strong melody note (Example 4–10).

It is possible to have consecutive chromatic approach notes. For this to occur, both must move in the same direction to the target note. See Example 4–11.

Example 4–9. *Scale-approach notes*

Bb is scale degree 4 of F major 7; G is scale degree 2 of F major 7; C is scale degree 4 of G–7; D is scale degree 2 of C7.

Example 4–10. *Chromatic-approach notes*

Example 4–11. *Consecutive chromatic-approach notes*

Example 4–12. *Surround tones*

Example 4–13. *Neighbor tones*

Surround Tones

When consecutive notes approach a target note from opposite directions, they are called **surround tones**. They can be both chromatic, both scale, or one of each (Example 4–12).

Neighbor Tones

A **neighbor tone** has the distinctive property of moving away from and then back to the same note. Neighbor tones can move by half step or whole step and are classified as either scale or chromatic. Example 4–13 shows a passage containing neighbor tones.

MELODY: RANGES AND INSTRUMENTATION

The range of a melody and the instrument(s) playing it must both be considered before starting to write. Certainly, any wind instrument can take the melody, regardless of range, when accompanied only by the rhythm section. However, when playing a lead line accompanied by other horns, the issue of balance comes into play. As discussed in Chapter 1, this is why it is critical to possess a strong knowledge of instrument ranges and tonal properties. Certainly, situations will occasionally arise in which a number of possibilities may exist, yet it is advantageous initially to establish and adhere to general guidelines regarding melody playing.

For lead playing accompanied by other horns, any *concert-pitched* melody that lies within the staff of the treble clef is in a suitable range for trumpet, soprano saxophone, and alto saxophone. The clarinet and flute both have beautiful sound within the scope of the treble clef. However, they could present potential balance problems when combined with other horns. For both clarinet and flute, the strong area for melody playing in an ensemble of horns would begin around the middle of the treble clef and continue up for an octave or more, depending on the context of the situation. At the bottom of the treble clef and below, the lower pitched instruments would naturally be the the more appropriate choices for lead playing. Example 4–14 shows a *concert-pitched* melody notated first within the staff of the treble clef and a second time an octave lower in the bass clef. The example also lists the instruments most likely to perform these lines.

Above the treble clef, the ever-increasing projection of the trumpet will affect the balance of a harmonized passage. In addition, the alto saxophone would be in the very top of its practical range, not the most appropriate area in which to lead a horn section. The particular tonal quality of the soprano saxophone, on the other hand, can be effective and appealing in melodies that rise to a fifth or so above the treble clef. The instrument choices for melody playing increase significantly if the *concert-pitched* lead line is in the lower half of the treble clef, below it, or completely in the bass clef. Example 4–15 contains further generalized information in order to provide an overall perspective with respect to appropriate instrumental timbres and ranges for melodies. How high is too high? How low is too low?

Example 4–14. *A concert-pitched melody in the treble clef and an octave lower*

TRUMPET, SOPRANO/ALTO SAXOPHONES: The melody lies completely within the treble clef, an ideal situation for lead playing by these instruments. All dynamic levels are possible.

CLARINET: This melody could be taken by the clarinet, but is low enough for the choice of accompanying horn(s) to be significant.

TENOR/BARITONE SAXOPHONES: This is a good melody range for both saxophones. All dynamic levels are possible. Because the two saxophones differ in timbre and projection, the particular accompanying horn(s) are significant.

TROMBONE: Although this melody is suitable for solo playing by the trombone, the first part of the line is low if the trombone is accompanied by other horn(s). The upper range of the trombone is the most effective one for lead playing.

Example 4–15. *Instrumental timbres and ranges for melodies*

TRUMPET: Suitable for trumpet, although somewhat high. The supporting instruments and resulting balance should be considered. The quietest dynamics would not be practical.

SOPRANO SAXOPHONE: Good range. All dynamics are possible.

CLARINET, FLUTE: Good range for both instruments, although flute is still low enough to be covered up and clarinet does not have the same fullness of sound as soprano saxophone in this range.

ALTO/TENOR SAXOPHONES: Ideal for both horns.

TRUMPET: All right if unaccompanied melody. Too low if played with other horns.

CLARINET: Luscious solo range for clarinet. Too low if accompanied by other horns.

TROMBONE, HORN: Excellent range for both instruments. All except the quietest dynamics are possible. With appropriate instrument choices, one or more horns can harmonize below.

BARITONE SAXOPHONE: Good range for lead playing. It is important to remember that, for such a large instrument, the baritone saxophone does not have the overall carrying power of the other saxophones.

TROMBONE: Low and not the best area for lead playing.

TUBA: Ideal range for solo tuba. Because the line approaches the top of the tuba range, the sound will project significantly.

EXERCISES

1. Modify the following melodies twice. In each case, add syncopation and make them swing. The two new versions of each melody should not be overly similar—each should have enough modifications so that they have individual personalities.

2. In each of the following melodies label all chord tones and extensions, identify all passing tones, and analyze all approach notes.

5

THE RHYTHM SECTION

The players in the rhythm section perform as a unit, individually, or in various combinations among themselves or with other members of an ensemble. Although its players are often assigned other roles, the essential functions of the rhythm section are:

1. keeping time

2. defining the harmony (chord progression)

3. generating the energy in an ensemble and executing the rhythmic patterns of the specific music styles being played

The chords in a progression are often called the *changes*. The playing of the changes by a pianist, guitarist, or vibraphonist is called *comping*. The unit of piano, bass, and drums represents the classic jazz trio. The guitar or vibraphone sometimes takes the place of piano; it is also common to have the three comping instruments in various combinations. In certain styles of music, electric keyboards and electric bass are more appropriate than the acoustic instruments. For projection and balance, jazz musicians play the electric guitar almost exclusively rather than the acoustic model.

GENERAL NOTATIONAL PRACTICE

Slash Notation

The simplest way to notate any rhythm-section instrument is to give it a part with slashes representing the individual beats in the time signature. These slashes are placed in the center of the staff. For piano, guitar, bass, and vibraphone, the chords are added above the slashes. The style of music—swing, bossa nova, etc.—is indicated in writing at the beginning of the part. With this type of notation, illustrated in Example 5–1, the players react to the music as they progress through the chart.

Note-head Shapes

Rhythm-section parts are rarely just slashes and chords for a whole arrangement. In their individual capacities, rhythm-section instruments can be given lead lines or other important melodic material, voiced in harmony with any of the horns or assigned solos. Arrangers use special note-head shapes when they want parts played in specific rhythms (Example 5–2). The particular manner in which these note heads are applied to the instruments will be illustrated in the examples throughout this chapter.

Example 5–1. *Slash notation*

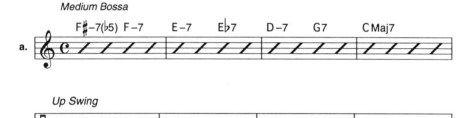

Example 5–2. *The use of note-head shapes*

Short-slash note heads are used with active lines for indefinitely pitched percussion instruments that come in different sizes.

Long-slash note heads, located on a staff's middle line, are used to specify rhythms for chording instruments. The diamond-shaped note heads are used for half notes and whole notes in any situation.

The X-shaped note-heads are generally used for cymbal parts (see DRUMS below). However, an arranger may specify the X-shaped note heads for any instrument.

Example 5–3. *Identical piano and guitar parts*

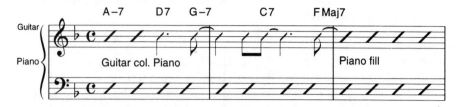

Sharing Lines in the Score

On the rare occasion that both the guitar and piano are just comping the changes for a whole arrangement—i.e., the instruments have identical parts without any individually notated passages—a separate line for guitar is not required *in the score*. In this situation only, the guitar can be listed next to the top piano line with the instruction *"col. piano"* ("with the piano"). Similarly, if the bass and piano are both just comping the changes, the direction "col. piano" may be indicated on the bass part. In these cases, the changes need only be indicated on the piano part *in the score* (Example 5–3).

DRUMS

Single-line drum parts will have slashes representing the beats alternating with rhythmic figures (Example 5–4a). In one of the most useful and common methods of drum notation, a line sits on top of the staff and indicates the important accents and punches as the music progresses, while the slashes within the staff function as a visual metronome track. This gives the drummer freedom to interpret within the framework of the music and to decide which drums or cymbals to play (Example 5–4b).

If an arranger wants figures played on specific pieces of the drum set, then different areas of the staff can represent the various components. The standard procedure is to assign the top line or space to the cymbals, the middle line(s) or space(s) to the snare drum or tom toms, and the bottom space to the bass drum. Initially, it is advisable to indicate in writing which lines and spaces represent which pieces of the drum set (Example 5–5).

Example 5–4. *Drum notation*

Example 5–5. *Notation for specific pieces of the drum set*

Medium Bossa

Ride cymbal

Bass drum

BASS

If the drums are the heart of an ensemble, then the bass is the pulse. A bass line spells out the individual chords in a progression and does so in a rhythm that defines the style of music.

Swing/Walking Bass

Swing passages in $\frac{4}{4}$ at any tempo use a walking bass line—one note per beat. In the simplest form of walking bass, the root falls on the first beat of the bar and at any point where the harmony changes (Example 5–6a). The remaining beats take chord tones (Example 5–6b).

Passing tones and approach notes may be added and are effective in walking bass lines. When the harmony changes, it is best to move stepwise to the new chord unless the line is going from root to root (Example 5–7).

Example 5–6. *Walking bass: simplest form*

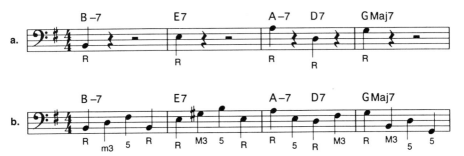

Example 5–7. *Walking bass with passing tones and approach notes*

Bass lines are often structured to coordinate properly with important melodic rhythms and accents. In these cases it is usually necessary to alter the strict note-per-beat pattern (Example 5–8).

The principles of walking-bass lines in $\frac{3}{4}$ are the same as those in $\frac{4}{4}$ time—the root falls on the first beat of a bar and when the harmony changes. Use stepwise motion to a new chord unless going from root to root (Example 5–9).

Latin

There is a vast array of Latin music styles throughout the world. Enough recorded and documented sources exist so that arrangers can research the authentic characteristics of a particular style when necessary. However, there are two types of Latin music, **bossa nova** and **samba**, that should be routinely familiar to contemporary arrangers. Bass lines for these styles center around the roots and fifths of the chords in a progression (Example 5–10).

Example 5–8. *Alteration of the strict note-per-beat pattern*

Example 5–9. *Walking bass in $\frac{3}{4}$*

Example 5–10. *Bass lines in bossa nova and samba*

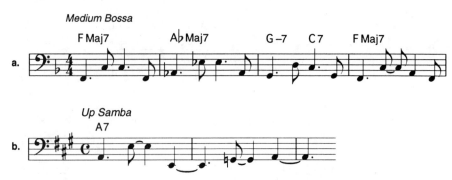

Example 5–11. *Bass lines in funk and soul*

Rock, Funk, Soul

Bass lines in any popular- or commercial-music style are usually performed on an electric bass. Styles of rock and related music—e.g., funk, soul, etc.—are plentiful. Although there are no definitive patterns for these genres, their bass lines tend to be busy and sixteenth-note oriented (Example 5–11).

PIANO

Although the guitar has had a profound and widespread influence on modern music, the piano remains the universally standard chordal instrument in the rhythm sections of jazz and other contemporary ensembles. As a first step to writing for the piano, it is very important to examine fundamental voicing methods.

Basic Voice Leading/Piano Technique

The process of advancing from one vertical structure to the next is called *voice leading*. The intervalic distance between the roots of successive chords is called the *root movement*. Even when chords are inverted, the root movement is determined by the interval between their roots. For example, the root movement between the chords A7 and DMaj7 is a perfect fifth (A down to D), regardless of inversion.

As a first step to acquiring voice-leading technique, work with closed voicings only and create *concerted* passages (the lead line is harmonized note-for-note and all the parts move in identical rhythm and direction). *In basic voice leading, common tones hold over in the same voice from one chord to the next and the remaining notes move to the nearest subsequent chord tones.* In diatonic passages, common tones will be present when the root movement between any two chords is the distance of a third, fourth, or fifth. In this manner of voice leading, the melody almost always moves by step. Musicians with limited keyboard proficiency can use this method to play through chord progressions. Example 5–12 illustrates common-tone voice leading.

With root movement of a second or third, parallel motion is acceptable, although common tones might be present. Voice leading may be common tone, parallel motion, or both. With root movement of a third, the melody will move by more than a step when parallel motion is chosen. Example 5–13 illustrates passages that move in parallel motion.

Example 5–12. *Common-tone voice leading*

a. Common tones hold from chord to chord in the same voice. Remaining tones move stepwise to the nearest tones in the following chord.

b. In four-part writing with triads, double the lead at the octave and use the same voice-leading method.

c. Use the same voice-leading method for chords with sevenths.

d. In four-part writing containing both triads and chords with sevenths, use the same voice-leading method. In the triads, double the root or fifth at the unison or octave.

Example 5–13. *Parallel motion*

Passages (a) and (b) use parallel motion only.

In passage (b), melody moves more than a step with root movement of a third.

Passage (c) contains stepwise melody only, despite root movement of a third.

Passage (d) contains root movement of a third and a combination of common tone/parallel motion.

It is not necessary to adhere to basic voice leading within the duration of a chord (Example 5–14a) after a cadence to a I chord (Example 5–14b) and after a passage has been at rest for more than half a measure (Example 5–14c).

Example 5–14. *Situations in which it is not necessary to use basic voice leading*

Notational Methods

The multidimensional piano usually performs a variety of functions during the course of an arrangement. Consequently, a piano part can be designed in several ways:

- slashes and chords (Example 5–15a)

- chords with specified rhythmic patterns (Example 5–15b)

- specified voicings (Example 5–15c)

- melodic material and chords with or without specified rhythmic patterns (Example 5–15d)

- combinations of the above (Example 5–15e)

Example 5–15. *Piano parts*

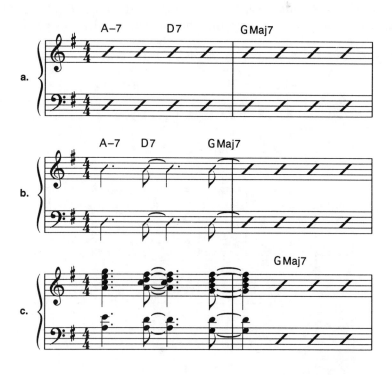

THE ELECTRIC GUITAR

The electric guitar is notated on a single staff and performs functions similar to those of the piano in the rhythm section. Because of the huge assortment of devices and effects available on the market, the electric guitar is capable of producing a variety of tonal qualities.

As a comping instrument, the guitar is the rhythm-section instrument most likely to have a part that is predominantly slashes and chords. Arrangers rarely write out chord voicings for guitar. It is important only to indicate specific rhythmic patterns when necessary. The guitar is also a strong melodic and soloing instrument and mixes well in soli passages with horns, either in unison or in harmony. Example 5–16 contains samples of typical guitar parts.

Example 5–16. *Guitar parts*

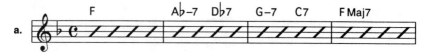

THE VIBRAPHONE

The vibraphone, like the guitar, performs the same functions as the piano in the rhythm section and has parts notated on a single staff. The vibraphone is an effective melodic and soloing instrument, and mixes well with horns in soli sections.

As with the other comping instruments, a vibraphone part may have slashes and chords only (Example 5–17a). Accomplished vibraphonists possess three- and four-mallet technique enabling them to play chords and multilayered passages. The presence in an ensemble of such a vibraphonist provides an arranger with more options when writing for this instrument (Example 5–17b).

Arrangers may occasionally desire the vibrato produced by the vibraphone when its motor is on and the paddles are rotating within the instrument's shafts. (Review, if necessary, the technical information on the vibraphone on pages 12–13.) In an arrangement, the written direction "motor on" *(fast, medium, or slow)* or "motor off" must appear at an appropriate point in the part giving the player time to flick the switch (Example 5–18).

Example 5–17. *Vibraphone parts*

Example 5–18. *Slow vibraphone vibrato*

MUSICAL DEVICES

Ostinato

An *ostinato* is a repeating motive or rhythmic pattern (Example 5–19). Ostinatos are usually assigned to one or more members of the rhythm section. Occasionally, one or more of the horns may perform an ostinato, either alone or in unison with one or more of the rhythm-section instruments.

Pedal

A *pedal*, sometimes called a *pedal point*, occurs in a chord progression when the same note is sustained in the lowest voice while the chords move. (Example 5–20).

Example 5–19. *Ostinatos*

Example 5–20. *Use of a pedal*

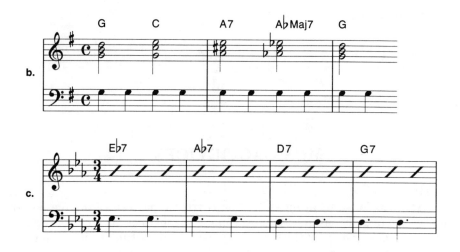

Vamp

The **vamp** is a type of intro in which a musical idea is repeated several times before the main body of music. The idea is usually the first chord or two of the opening chorus or the chords supporting an important motive in the chorus. Occasionally, a fragment of the opening motive is included. The vamp is played in rhythms that are the same as or similar to those in the music's first few measures. In a live performance, musicians can create impromptu introductions to musical selections by performing vamps. In an arrangement, the arranger may notate a vamp in the score and either (1) indicate a number of repetitions or (2) add the direction "open" so that the vamp is repeated indefinitely until the band director cues the beginning of the chart. Example 5–21 contains sample notated vamps.

Example 5–21. *Vamps*

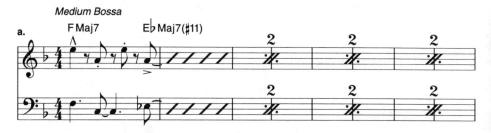

Occasionally, an arranger may choose to "vamp" harmonies or rhythms in a different way than the material in an arrangement's first chorus. This sets up the element of surprise and can be an effective opening. An arranger also has the option of restating any type of intro during the course of an arrangement to act as an interlude or to set up another statement of the main theme.

SCORE PRACTICE

The rhythm section is versatile in its functions as an accompanying unit and an independent ensemble. Example 5–22 illustrates typical rhythm section notation in score form.

Example 5–22. *Rhythm-section scores*

EXERCISES

1. Compose bass lines on the following chord progressions in the styles and time signatures indicated.

a. **SWING, $\frac{4}{4}$ and $\frac{3}{4}$**

Bb   B○7   / C–7   C#○7   / D–7   G7   / C–7   F7   /
F–7   Bb7   / Eb   Eb–   / Bb   F7   / Bb   /

b. **SWING, $\frac{4}{4}$ and $\frac{3}{4}$**

C   Eb7   / Ab Maj7   B7   / E Maj7   E7   / A Maj7   /

c. **SWING, $\frac{4}{4}$ and $\frac{3}{4}$**

F#–7(b5)   B7(b9)   / E–7   A7   / Ab–7   Db7   / Gb Maj7   /

d. **BOSSA NOVA, $\frac{4}{4}$**

G Maj7   / Bb Maj7   / G Maj7   / G–7   C7   /
F Maj7   / Ab Maj7   / A–7   D7   / G Maj7   /

e. **FUNK/ROCK, $\frac{4}{4}$**

E7   / A7   / B7   / E7   /

f. **SWING, $\frac{3}{4}$**

G–   / C–7   / G–   / D–7(b5)   G7(b9)   /
C–7   / C7   / F Maj7   /

g. **FUNK/ROCK, $\frac{4}{4}$**

A7   / D7   / G7   / C Maj7   /

h. **BOSSA NOVA, $\frac{4}{4}$**

A–7(b5)   D7(b9)   / G–7   C7   / B–7   E7   / A Maj7   /

2. Arrange each of the following passages for a rhythm section. In each case use the instrumentation listed and modify the melody to conform to the indicated musical style. (The melody may be shifted to another octave.) Include specific rhythmic figures for the instruments backing the melody. Do not compose an entire bass line unless indicated.

a. (LATIN/BOSSA NOVA) Guitar plays the melody accompanied by piano, bass, and drums. Compose the entire bass line.

b. (MEDIUM SWING) Bass plays the melody accompanied by piano and drums.

c. (MEDIUM BALLAD) Piano plays the melody accompanied by guitar, bass, and drums.

d. (UP SWING) Vibraphone and guitar play the melody accompanied by piano, bass, and drums. Compose the entire bass line.

6

TWO PARTS

In conventional modes of playing (no special techniques or effects), horns are single-line instruments that play one note at a time. When two or more horns play simultaneously, they create a body of sound resulting from two or more simultaneously played notes. The depth and scope of the sound broaden as the number of horns increases, the result at any instant being an interval or chord.

TWO-PART SOLI

There are three relationships between the movement of the parts:

1. Parts move in the same direction (***parallel motion***).

2. Parts move in opposite directions (***contrary motion***).

3. Some parts sustain while the others move (***independent motion***).

Example 6–1 illustrates these relationships.

In tonal music any arranged passage must accurately retain the flavor of the harmony. Even in the most sophisticated instances the music should, simply put, sound right. As pointed out in Chapter 5, harmonizing the lead line note

Example 6–1. *Movement of the parts*

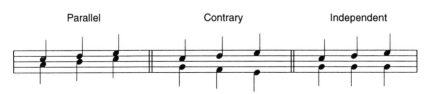

for note in identical rhythms is termed concerted writing. Intervals of a third or sixth are the most consonant intervals; therefore, it is beneficial to consider their importance before working with other spacings between parts. Because of the stability of thirds and sixths, passages using these intervals exclusively are technically sound. The operating procedure is uncomplicated: the distance between the two parts at any point will be a third or sixth, major or minor. Occasionally, the interval of a tenth—a third plus an octave—is a workable spacing if a melody is consistently high or a particular instrumental combination suggests its use. Using only thirds and sixths provides three possibilities:

1. The second line lies consistently a third (tenth) below the lead line.

2. The second line lies consistently a sixth below the lead line.

3. The second line lies in a combination of thirds and sixths below the lead line.

In Example 6–2, a line is harmonized several times to show the possibilities.

Example 6–2. *Several harmonizations of a melody*

If the harmony changes on an anticipated melody note, the new chord must also be anticipated. In a straight-ahead passage, the note chosen for the second part will belong to the new chord (Example 6–3).

A good rule of thumb is to make sure that the distance between notes in an underpart is not radically more than the distance between the corresponding notes in the lead line. This applies not only to two parts, but to any number of parts. Generally, the distance between notes in an underpart may be increased by as much as a minor third. Adhering to this principle will ensure a smooth flow in the voice leading. Larger discrepancies between parts will affect the cohesiveness of a passage, especially in two-part writing. There are three situations, however, to which this procedure does not necessarily apply:

1. When the lead line repeats or sustains the same note and the harmony does not change, an underpart can jump between different notes of the chord.

2. When the lead line repeats or sustains the same note and the harmony changes, an underpart can, within reason, move a greater distance.

3. If the chord progression is at rest, such as at the end of a phrase within a longer passage or on the final chord of a cadence, parts can move more within the duration of the chord.

The music of Example 6–4 illustrates various situations. The manner in which an arranger starts a passage influences the direction the music takes.

Example 6–3. *Melody and harmony are anticipated*

Example 6–4. *Comparison of strong and weak harmonizations*

Passage (b) is stronger; the second line reflects the character of the melody.

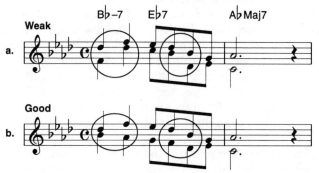

The G Maj7 chord represents a point of stability; in passage (c), the voice-leading principles have been relaxed within the duration of the chord. Passage (d) is the strongest passage.

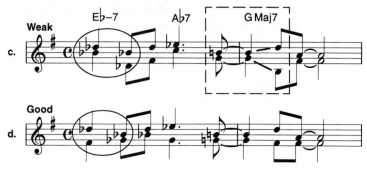

When using intervals other than thirds and sixths in two-part writing, the contour and rhythm of a melody are significant. It is important now to recognize strong melody notes on the stressed beats in any measure. Harmonizing these melody notes with notes a third or sixth below in the underpart retains the straightforwardness of the passage. This would place intervals other than thirds or sixths in the second line under less stressed parts of a melody. These other intervals serve as links between the stable consonant areas, and they should move—stepwise preferably or at least as close to stepwise as possible—to the interval of a third or sixth in either contrary or independent motion. Example 6–5 illustrates how incorporating intervals other than thirds or sixths can change the character of a passage.

Example 6–5. *Incorporating intervals other than thirds and sixths*

Adding sustain to the second part creates independent motion in the lead line. In addition, the sustain produces different spacing between parts. Example 6–6 illustrates the different results when the same melody is harmonized in two ways: (1) note for note and (2) with sustain in the second part.

In Example 6–7, the effect of sustained notes in a part is exhibited again, this time incorporating the larger intervals of a ninth and tenth.

Example 6–6. *Harmonizing note for note and with sustain in the second part*

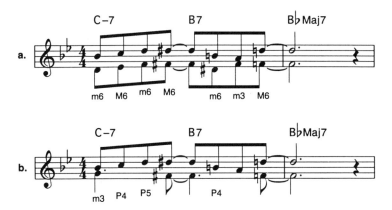

Example 6–7. *Sustained notes with compound intervals*

To this point examples have shown two-part writing with both parts notated on one staff. Example 6–8 shows a two-part passage as it would appear in a score: each line is notated on a different staff.

The manner in which an arranger initially shapes a melody influences how the second part is going to be treated. Thus far, two procedures for harmonizing melodies have been examined:

1. The lead line is harmonized note for note—concerted writing.

2. Sustain is added in the second part, creating instances of independent motion in the lead.

Some melodies or parts of melodies will present a possible third approach, that of adding notes in the second part (Example 6–9). This can be musically interesting in that it produces independent motion in the second line and often results in effective counterpoint. *When adding notes in the second line, determine the appropriateness of the extra notes and consider how the two parts will balance out.*

Example 6–8. *Two-part writing with each line notated on a separate staff*

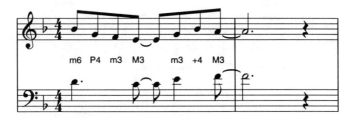

Example 6–9. *Adding notes in the second line*

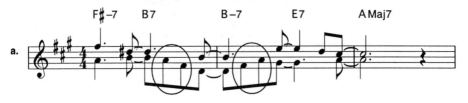

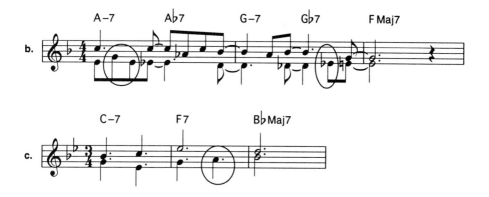

APPROACH-NOTE HARMONIZATION

In Chapter 4 various types of approach notes were discussed (pages 58–59). *An approach note in the lead line is usually supported by the same type of approach note in the second line.*

Scale Approaches

A scale approach note relates diatonically to the chord supporting its target note. Since major and minor scales are constructed in series of whole and half steps, it is possible that a diatonic scale approach that moves by half step can also function as a chromatic approach. Example 6–10 shows scale approaches in passages with diatonic chord progressions.

Example 6–10. *Scale approaches with diatonic chord progressions*

In the second measure of passage (b), instead of adding another harmony note under the D approach note in the melody, the G in the second part holds over resulting in independent and contrary motion.

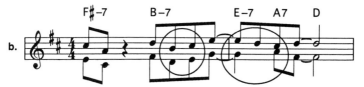

Scale approaches function optimally in diatonic situations. In this respect the harmony note supporting a scale approach to a nondiatonic chord may still belong to the preceding diatonic chord. In Example 6–11, scale approaches to notes on nondiatonic chords are circled.

Chromatic Approaches

A chromatic approach note always moves to its target note by half step. Therefore, the chromatic approach in the lead line, as well as the supporting chromatic approach in the second part, often do not belong to the chord of the target note. The passage in Example 6–12 contains chromatic approach notes and a diatonic chord progression.

In some cases a melodic half step is analyzable as a scale approach in addition to a chromatic approach. Either analysis will usually apply appropriately to the passage, the arranger deciding which particular sound he or she desires at the time. Example 6–13 illustrates this situation. The passages in Example 6–14 contain chromatic approach notes. The chord progressions are not completely diatonic.

Example 6–11. *Scale approaches to notes of nondiatonic chords*

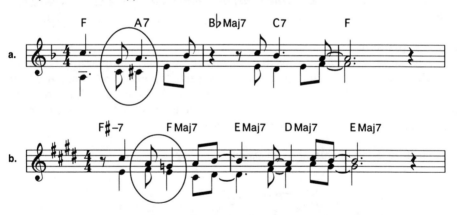

Example 6–12. *Chromatic approach notes with a diatonic chord progression*

Example 6–13. *Both a scale approach and a chromatic approach*

Example 6–14. *Chromatic approach notes with partially chromatic progressions*

a.

b.

Consecutive Approaches

Consecutive approach notes in a lead line are harmonized in the same manner as individual approach notes. Therefore, consecutive approach notes in the second part function similarly to the notes they are supporting. Example 6–15 illustrates this.

Example 6–15. *Consecutive approach notes*

a. Consecutive chromatic approaches

b. Surround tones

Example 6–16. *Neighbor tones*

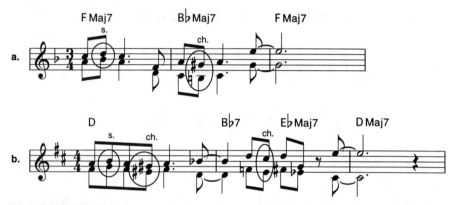

Neighbor Tones

Neighbor tones move away from and back to the same note. They can have scale or chromatic function and are harmonized accordingly (Example 6–16).

GUIDE-TONE LINES

A useful method of harmonizing a lead line is that of constructing a second line based around the guide tones in the chords of the progression. In creating the second part, choose the guide tones first. Other notes may be added and the rhythm varied to make the line more interesting. Example 6–17 illustrates the procedure.

Example 6–17. *Constructing a second line using guide tones*

Step 1: Assign 3rds or 7ths (sometimes 5ths) to the second part. The movement should be stepwise or by common tone. The line may skip from one guide tone to the other within the duration of a chord.

Step 2: Embellish the guide-tone line to conform with the melody.

UNISONS

As with harmonized music, an arranger's inner ear is very important when creating unison passages. [*With respect to arranging, "unison passages" will represent instruments in octaves, as well as unisons.*] Instruments produce different timbres and varying degrees of sound penetration in the different parts of their ranges. Because the lead line in a unison is being duplicated by one or more instruments, the choice of instruments will define the impact of the resulting passage. Two-horn arrangements present the following possible unison combinations:

1. two horns

2. one horn and rhythm-section instrument(s)

3. two horns and rhythm-section instrument(s)

4. two or more rhythm-section instruments.

Unison writing can enhance passages when alternated with harmonized parts. Using unisons and either harmonizing only isolated notes at strategic points or just the final note of a passage can also be effective. Example 6–18 shows several possible ways to double a melody and provides suggestions of which instruments would be the most likely ones to play the respective lines. If this melodic fragment were higher or lower, the possible combinations would change. Even though harmonies are absent, the issue of balance in unison passages is important.

Example 6–18. *Doubling a melody*

Clarinet, Trumpet, Flugelhorn, Soprano Sax, Alto Sax, Elec. Guitar

Tenor Sax, Baritone Sax, Horn, Trombone, Clarinet, Bass Clarinet, Elec. Guitar

Baritone Sax, Trombone, Bass Trombone, Tuba, Double Bass, Elec. Bass

ADDITIONAL VOICING PROCEDURES

It is not necessary for intervals other than thirds and sixths always to function as subordinate sounds. The other intervals can be very effective and attractive when used on the *stressed* parts of melodies. Of course, the context of the situation and the resulting musical impact remain a consideration—the music should not sound contrived.

Some situations initially suggest the possibility of supporting the more dissonant intervals. For example, musical passages that are very rhythmic or that have isolated attacks, often called ***punches***, can accommodate varying degrees of dissonance. The issue of perspective is important here. In long-flowing passages or sustained lines, the dissonant impact will be more fully emphasized, and an arranger must be certain that this is the desired effect. In shorter bursts and rhythmically active music, the "buzz" obtained with dissonant spacing remains, but it is not as blatant within the overall texture of a passage. Often, horn passages with some degree of dissonance in them are excellent as background lines. Fourths and fifths, consonant intervals with a more open sound, are good choices for emphasizing and adding some bite to the ends of phrases. In any event the nonstraightforward use of intervals should supplement basic arranging technique. Example 6–19 presents three passages that contain alternative voicings at strategic points in the lines.

Example 6–19. *Alternate voicings*

Parallel Seconds and Fourths

An interesting and often appealing procedure is the use of parallel spacing (Example 6–20). Successions of seconds and fourths yield distinctively interesting results, if not used excessively. (Voicings in fourths and other special voicings will be discussed in depth in Chapter 8.)

Example 6–20. *The use of parallel spacing*

BACKGROUNDS

Although improvisation is a primary feature of jazz, most contemporary genres of music include improvisation in varying degrees. Soloing passages are often showcased in arrangements. Interesting and complementary background lines behind a soloist are important components of arrangements. When there are two horns an arranger has some options when creating accompaniment for a soloist:

1. A horn soloist improvises on the changes accompanied by the rhythm section only. A capable rhythm section should create ample excitement and interest by playing the changes, generating the feel of the music, and reacting to the soloist.

2. Backgrounds are played by one horn, or both horns if a rhythm section instrument is soloing. If two horns are playing, the background line can be a unison, an octave, harmonized, alternated between horns, or any combination of these.

3. The soloist performs without any accompaniment—the rest of the band *lays out*.

4. Any combination of the above. If an arrangement has more than one soloing section, each section can have its own distinctive background features.

A background has its name because of what it does—it remains in the background. It is a lead line that has a specific function. It could be anything: a few sustained notes, short melodic fragments, punches, or even another melody that acts as a counterpoint to the improvised lines of the soloist. Whatever shape the background takes, it must befit the musical situation and enhance the soloist's efforts. Backgrounds can be unisons or harmonized lines and can use any two-part arranging methods.

Guide-tone Backgrounds

One procedure that is a common and useful option in creating backgrounds is that of basing a background passage around the guide tones from the chords in a progression. This method differs from the one discussed—harmonizing a lead line with a second line based on guide tones—because now *both* parts are created around the guide tones, which are always the third and seventh, and sometimes the fifth in any chord. The distance between the third and seventh of a chord is some variation of the interval of a fourth, either perfect, raised (a tritone), or inverted (a fifth). Therefore, employing guide tones as a focal point for a musical passage is another useful application of intervals other than thirds and sixths. The distinction here is that the guide tones are the defining notes of any chord. The intervals outline the harmony clearly and are pleasing to the ear. An arranger can use the guide tones alone or add other notes to make a more involved line. In any event the initial placement of the guide tones will determine beforehand the general contour of the resulting background passage. Example 6–21 provides an idea of how to work with the guide tones in creating a line.

Example 6–21. *The use of guide tones to create backgrounds*

Each instrument is given one of the guide tones from each chord in the progression.

The lines can be modified. They must all center around the guide tones.

The guide tones have switched parts and the lines are modified; this passage is higher in range than the two preceding passages.

SCORE PRACTICE

The next three examples show sample two-horn scores. In Example 6–22, the score is pitched in concert (nontransposed)—the transposing horns are in the same key as the rhythm section. Example 6–23 exhibits the same score as it would look transposed. In this case the horns have been transposed to the keys and pitches as they would appear on their respective parts. Finally, Example 6–24 illustrates a two-horn background for a guitar solo in a concert pitched score.

Example 6–22. *Concert score: trumpet and alto saxophone notated where they sound*

Example 6–23. *Transposed score: trumpet and alto saxophone notated as they would appear on their respective parts*

Try It Like This

Norman David

Example 6–24. *Concert score: guitar solo with the two horns playing a background line derived primarily from guide tones*

EXERCISES

1. Add second parts in concerted rhythm to the following melodies. Use only combinations of thirds and sixths between parts.

a.

b.

2. Harmonize each of the following melodies with an embellished guide-tone line.

a.

b.

3. Harmonize the following melodies using any available method.

a.

b.

4. Harmonize the following melodies using spacing as indicated.

a. Place seconds at points marked with asterisks.

b. Harmonize using only parallel fourths.

5. Create guide-tone background lines on the following chord progressions.

a. A–7(♭5)   D7(♭9)   **/** G–7   C7   **/** F–7   B♭7   **/** E♭ Maj7   **/**

b. B7   E7   **/** A7   D7   **/** G–7   C7   **/** F Maj7   **/**

c. C Maj7   D♭7   **/** G♭ Maj7   B7   **/** E Maj7   G7   **/** C Maj7   **/**

6. Score the following melody for alto saxophone, trombone, piano, guitar, double bass, and drums.

7

THREE, FOUR, AND FIVE PARTS

FUNDAMENTAL METHODS

Close Voicings

Although voicings are comprised of either chord tones only or a combination of chord tones and extensions, it is logical to examine first those that contain chord tones only. When a chord tone is in the lead, a close voicing in three or four parts is completed by adding some or all of the remaining chord tones below the lead note. In a five-part close voicing, double the lead at the octave—i.e., double the lead at the octave in a four-note close voicing. Example 7–1 contains several typical close voicings.

Example 7–1. *Close voicings*

On three-part close triads, add the remaining chord tones below the lead. On three-part close with any type of seventh chord, have an outside interval of a sixth or seventh. On low melody notes, an outside interval of a fifth is acceptable.

On four-part close triads, the melody may be doubled at the unison or octave. On four-part close with any type of seventh chord, the remaining chord tones are placed below the lead.

In a five-part voicing with chord tones only, the lead is doubled an octave below—or above with an appropriate instrument such as flute, clarinet, or soprano sax.

Drop Two

In **_drop-two_** voicings, the second note in a close voicing is shifted an octave lower to the bottom of the structure. As a result the span of the voicing from top to bottom is wider and the relationships between voices have changed. Drop-two voicings are useful in three-, four-, and five-part writing (Example 7–2).

Drop Three

A **_drop-three_** voicing results when the third note in a close voicing is shifted an octave lower to the bottom of the structure. The resulting span is wider than that in a drop-two voicing. Drop-three voicings are applicable in four- and five-part writing (Example 7–3).

Example 7–2. *Drop-two voicings*

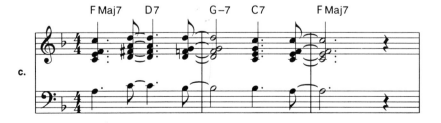

Example 7–3. *Drop-three voicings*

Drop Two and Four

In a ***drop-two-and-four*** voicing, the second and fourth notes in a close voicing are shifted an octave lower, as a unit in the same order, to the bottom of the structure. This voicing, having a wider span than a drop-three voicing, is useful in four-, and five-part writing (Example 7–4).

Example 7–4. *Drop-two-and-four voicings*

Melody Ranges for Drop Voicings

The configuration of a voicing changes with any of the drop methods. Example 7–5 presents suggested melody ranges for each method and shows how these ranges move a little higher as voicings become wider. Certainly, in some cases, depending on the instrumentation or musical context, the limits can be stretched somewhat either upward or downward. However, it will be possible to harmonize most melodies successfully using these guidelines.

Mixed Structures

When melodies are active or angular, it is often more practical to use mixed structures instead of a single drop method, unless complete parallel motion is intended. A combination of drop methods results in increased contrary and independent motion between parts (Example 7–6).

Example 7–5. *Melody ranges for drop voicings*

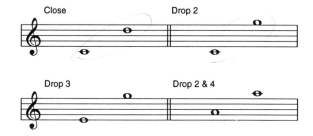

Example 7–6. *Contrary and independent motion in mixed structures*

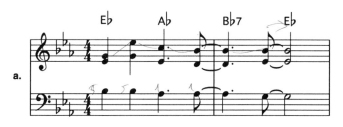

EXTENSIONS

General Practice

Resonance and depth of sound increase when extensions are added to voicings. Extensions, natural or altered, usually take the place of chord tones. When an extension is already in a melody, it automatically becomes part of the voicing. Otherwise, if an extension is indicated in a chord, it should be placed somewhere in the voicing. In some situations an extension can be included even if it is not in the melody or chord symbol; for instance, the ninth is frequently effective substituting for the root. Initially, it is beneficial to establish the following usage chart:

- 9, ♭9, and ♯9 replace the root

- 11 and ♯11 (♭5) replace 5

- 13 and ♭13 (♯5) replace 5.

Three and Four Parts

Extensions should be added to a voicing in a manner that does not obscure the intended chord sound. Because the identity of any vertical structure is based in its foundation, *enough of the basic chord sound should be situated in the bottom end to support whatever other notes, chord tone or extension, are above.* Effective voicings in the horns will complement what the rhythm section is playing; the bassist will generally supply roots when necessary with more complex harmonies. Example 7–7 displays some three- and four-part voicings, each containing one extension. The two short motives in Example 7–8 illustrate three- and four-part writing in which extensions and various drop voicings are used.

Example 7–7. *Three- and four-part closed voicings with a single extension*

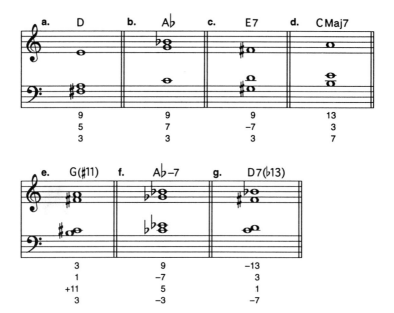

Example 7–8. *Three- and four- part passages with extensions and drop voicings*

Five Parts

The addition of an extension to a five-part closed voicing creates a fairly dense structure because five notes are grouped together within the span of an octave. Two or more successive seconds will occur between parts. Unless the intensity of seconds is intended (see SPACING, on pages 113–14 and CLUSTERS, on pages 128–31), it will probably be more appropriate to create a five-part structure that spans more than one octave. In many cases simply expanding the outside interval just one step to a ninth (often by drop two) will produce a useful five-part voicing that will essentially sound like a closed structure. In any event there are two ways to add one extension to a five-part voicing, whether it is close or not:

1. When the lead note is an unaltered extension, double it at the octave; add chord tones for the remainder of the voicing (Example 7–9a, b, c).

2. When a chord tone is in the lead and the melody is not too active, add an extension in place of the octave doubling to create a structure with five different notes (Example 7–9d, e).

Five-part voicings with the lead doubled are effective in faster lines (Example 7–10a). Voicings with five different notes lend themselves more to slower, sustained music or to percussive situations (Example 7–10b). At times, both procedures can be used within the same passage (Example 7–10c). Adding two or three extensions to a five-part voicing produces colorful sonorities. (Dense or special structures result when three extensions are used—see ALTERED EXTENSION COMBINATIONS, page 115, and UPPER STRUCTURES on pages 131–33.) It is beneficial to keep one, if not both, of the guide tones in the voicing. Example 7–11 illustrates how two extensions can be added to five-part voicings.

Example 7–9. *Five-part voicings with a single extension*

Example 7–10. *Some uses for five-part voicings*

a. Double lead on active line

b. Five different notes on nonactive line

c. Combining of double-lead and five-note voicings

Example 7–11. *Five-part voicings with two extensions*

INDEPENDENT LEAD

Independent lead writing is effective in both small and large ensembles. With three or more horns the melody moves while the underparts are voiced as a separate unit in more sustained harmonies. Independent lead provides an alternative and interesting way in which to voice a passage. It can also be the most feasible method when working with melodies that otherwise would be difficult to harmonize note for note (Example 7–12).

Example 7–12. *Independent lead writing*

APPROACH-NOTE HARMONIZATION

The proper harmonization of approach notes will add strength and vitality to an arrangement. As with two-part writing, there will be instances when there is more than one choice in deciding which type of approach harmony to use. Although variances in sound between the different types of approach harmonies can be subtle at any tempo or even indiscernible at faster tempos, the strong treatment of approach patterns ensures a perceived naturalness or correctness in an arranged passage.

Scale, Chromatic, Neighbor

The harmonization procedures for scale, chromatic, and neighbor approach notes with three to five parts are identical to those with two-part writing (Example 7–13).

Example 7–13. *Three-to five-part voicings with scale, chromatic, and neighbor approaches*

Harmonized scale approach notes.

Harmonized chromatic approach notes.

Harmonized neighbor tones.

Harmonized surround tones.

Dominant Reharmonization

Another method of treating approach notes is that of forming a dominant harmony. When applicable, an approach note in a lead line is harmonized to produce the V7 of the chord supporting the target note (Example 7–14).

Example 7–14. *Dominant harmony on approach notes*

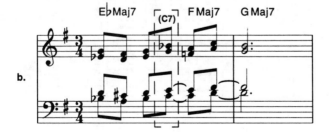

UNISONS

Small ensembles will have some combination of woodwind and/or brass instruments. A unison passage for three to five horns (with or without rhythm-section instruments) will almost always be written as either a true unison or in octaves. Double octaves would likely produce an unbalanced sound because either the highs or the lows would dominate. Occasionally, when there are five horns and one of them is low-pitched. double octaves might work. (Chapter 11 will include a discussion of unisons for sections of four or five woodwinds or brass.) When writing a unison for a small group of horns, the best procedure is to use a true unison when all the horns are high-pitched and to place all the instruments in their strongest registers when there is a combination of high- and low-pitched horns. Example 7–15 shows some typical small-ensemble unisons.

Example 7–15. *Small-ensemble unisons*

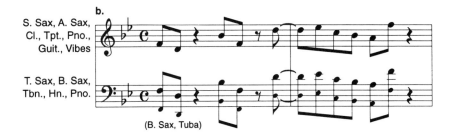

VOICING CONSIDERATIONS

The indiscriminate placement of notes can hinder the effectiveness of a voicing. Thus, it is necessary to look at some harmonically related applications.

Placement of the Lowest Note

Depending on its function in the harmony, the lowest note of a voicing, if placed too low, can cloud up the intended chord sound. Unless the bottom note in a voicing is the root or fifth of the chord, it is reasonable to establish the lower limits as D in the middle of the bass clef for the other chord tones and E in the middle of the bass clef for extensions. This may be stretched lower on occasion as long as the harmonic clarity of a passage is maintained. If the bottom note is the fifth of the chord, it can safely be placed at least as low as the first F below the bass clef. The root of a chord can be as far down in a voicing as desired. *Since the configuration of a voicing changes from method to method, dropping a voice can produce a structure in which the new bottom note is inappropriately low*. Example 7–16 illustrates several situations.

Example 7–16. *Lowest-note placement*

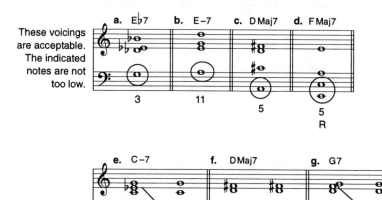

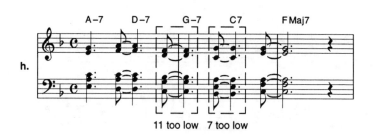

When ♭5 is indicated in a dominant chord, it may be the lowest note of a voicing because its implied sound will be the root of the related sub-V7 chord (e.g., an E7(♭5) chord with a B♭ on the bottom will resemble B♭7). This principle applies to any voicing configuration. If the lowered fifth is in a dominant chord that is part of a II-V progression, the flatted fifth in the bass will form a smooth chromatic link between the roots of the preceding II chord and the following I chord (Example 7–17).

Spacing

The spacing between notes, adjacent or otherwise, determines the strength and character of a vertical structure.

- Be cautious when placing steps, half or whole, between the two highest voices. Used imprudently, seconds will stand out and offset the balance of a passage. If seconds between the two highest voices in a harmonized passage are intended, the best results are obtained when they are brief in duration, placed on upbeats or unstressed parts of a melody, and approached and left in contrary motion. Placing a second on the downbeat or stressed part of a melody emphasizes the "buzz" it produces at the top of a voicing (Example 7–18).

- As a rule, tritones should be avoided between the highest two voices. Occasionally, in a diminished pattern or cadential situation, a tritone may be placed at the top of the voicing in a diminished or dominant chord. In these cases the tritone should be resolved on the subsequent voicing (Example 7–19). In any event, never place consecutive tritones in the highest two voices.

- Although the very dissonant interval of a minor ninth should fundamentally be avoided between any two voices, it remains available in two chordal situations:

Example 7-17. *♭5 in the bass*

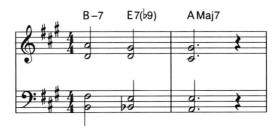

1. When ♭9 in a dominant chord is in the lead, the root can be placed below it (Example 7–20a). When ♭9 is not in the lead, it should take the place of the root.

2. Unless it is in the lead, ♭5 can be placed above the fourth in a minor 7(♭5) chord (Example 7–20b).

Example 7–18. *Seconds on the downbeats*

Example 7–19. *A tritone at the top of the voicing*

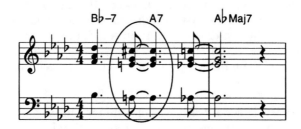

Example 7–20. *The minor ninth*

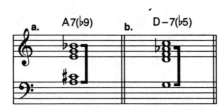

Altered-Extension Combinations

In five-part writing, some combinations of chord tones and altered exten-sions, when applicable, produce rich harmonies.

- Do not combine ♮5 with either ♭5 or ♯5 in the same voicing. However:

  1. If ♯11 is in a chord and in the lead, 5 can be placed below it (Example 7–21a).

  2. If ♯11 is in a chord and in the lead, 13 can be placed below it; but *omit the fifth from the voicing* (Example 7–21b).

- Do not combine ♮9 with either ♭9 or ♯9 . However, ♭9 and ♯9 in the same voicing are a workable combination when one of them is in the lead. The third of the chord must be below the ♯9 in order to avoid the inter-val of a minor ninth. The ♭13 works in combination with either or both of the altered ninths (Example 7–21c).

In Example 7–22, a short motive is voiced in five parts. Each of the three notes in the motive is harmonized using a different spacing and combination of chord tones and extensions. Because of careful planning, the voicings are logi-cal and the voice leading flows smoothly.

Example 7–21. *Combinations of chord tones and altered extensions*

Example 7–22. *Different spacing and different combinations of chord tones and extensions*

SCORE PRACTICE

Segments of two arrangements are now illustrated in full-score format. The first passage features a unison melody for alto sax and trumpet, with close-voicing background chords for tenor sax, baritone sax, and trombone (Example 7–23a). The second passage has a melody in the trumpet harmonized with alto sax, tenor sax, and trombone, primarily in drop-two voicings (Example 7–23b).

Example 7–23. *Full-score format*

EXERCISES

1. Voice the following line in close position for three, four, and five horns.

2. The following are either drop-two, drop-three, or drop-two-and-four voicings. In each case give the letter name of the chord, identify the particular drop method being used, and notate the chord in its original close position.

3. Harmonize the following melodies in concerted rhythms (identical rhythms in all voices) for the number of horns indicated plus a rhythm section of piano, bass, and drums. Use a variety of voicing methods and approach-note harmonizations.

a. (3, 4 horns)

b. (3, 4 horns)

c. (4, 5 horns)

d. (3, 4, 5 horns)

4. Score the following melodies as unisons (octaves) for the indicated horns and rhythm section.

a. (alto sax, tenor sax, trumpet)

b. (alto sax, baritone sax, trumpet, trombone)

c. (alto sax, tenor sax, baritone sax, trumpet, trombone)

5. Score the following melodies for the number of horns indicated plus rhythm section. In each case, have as much independent lead as possible. Use a variety of voicing methods and approach-note harmonizations.

a. (3 horns)

b. (4 horns)

c. (4 horns)

d. (4 horns)

d. (5 horns: five parts, no doubled voices)

e. (5 horns: double a voice)

8

SPECIAL VOICINGS

Certain voicings have configurations based on a specific interval or harmonic principle. These voicings are:

1. voicings in fourths

2. spreads

3. clusters

4. upper structures

Because of their distinctive configurations and sounds, these special voicings do not function optimally in fast or busy passages. Their strength and effectiveness are born out in some or all of the following situations:

• Percussive passages

• Backgrounds

• High or low points of phrases

• Ends of phrases

• Sustained passages

The upcoming discussions of special voicings will explain their methods of construction and most useful applications. Familiarity with timbre properties of band instruments is critical with respect to these voicings. It is helpful to play on the piano any examples—those in this text and those created during the course of study—to get initial perceptions of their particular sonorities. Ultimately, the most valuable aural impressions of special voicings are gained from hearing them played by different combinations of instruments.

VOICINGS IN FOURTHS

In a *voicing in fourths*, the predominant interval between any pair of adjacent notes is a fourth. The wider spacing in this type of voicing produces an open, ringing sonority—a distinctive alternative to the familiar cohesiveness of a structure derived from a close voicing.

In a voicing in fourths all the notes must belong to the underlying chord. Although the procedures for three, four, and five parts are similar, note the following:

Three Parts
- Voicing down from the lead note, all intervals *must* be perfect or augmented fourths. Do not place any thirds within the structure.

- Not all chord tones will be present, but the basic chord should be reasonably discernible.

- The guideline for lowest-note placement should be observed.

Example 8–1 illustrates sample three-part voicings in fourths.

Four / Five Parts
- Voicing down from the lead note, all intervals should be perfect or augmented fourths.

- With four parts, a major third may be placed between the highest two voices.

- With five parts, a major third, minor third, or perfect fifth is acceptable anywhere within the structure. In five-part voicings containing one or more altered extensions, two intervals of a third may occur.

Example 8–1. *Three-part voicings in fourths*

- Adjacent thirds, doubled notes, or minor ninth intervals should not be placed within the voicing. (With six or more parts, doubled notes together with one of the accepted minor ninth intervals could be used.)

- All chord tones need not be present as long as enough of the basic chord is discernible.

- With dominant chords, the tritone should be within the voicing. Also, ♭5 in a dominant chord can be placed as low as desired in a voicing in fourths (see PLACEMENT OF THE LOWEST NOTE on pages 112–13).

- Observe the guideline for lowest-note placement.

Example 8–2 illustrates sample four- and five-part voicings in fourths.

For the most effective results when using voicings in fourths, it is helpful to work with the practical melody ranges proposed in Example 8–3.

Example 8–2. *Four- and five-part voicings in fourths*

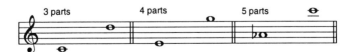

Example 8–3. *Practical lead ranges for voicings in fourths*

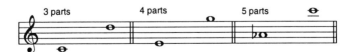

When a II–7 chord is voiced in fourths, ♮11 may be the bottom note in the voicing, regardless of how low it is (Example 8–4). The implied sound is the root of the related V7(sus4) chord. For example, a B–7 chord with E on the bottom will resemble and function like E7(sus4).

Voicings in fourths work well in both nonactive and percussive passages (Example 8–5). Whether they be principle thematic material or a background behind a soloist, lines voiced in fourths will add verve to the music if they are not overused.

Example 8–4. *Voicing a II–7 chord in fourths*

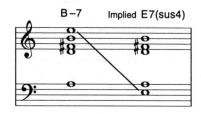

Example 8–5. *Voicings in fourths in both nonactive and percussive passages*

SPREADS

A *spread* is a voicing that can span two octaves or more. In a spread voicing the root of the chord is always on the bottom of the structure, the only exception occurring when an inversion is specified. Though the procedures for four and five parts are similar, note the following:

Four Parts
- The bottom note is the root (except for inversions).

- Guide tones are placed in the two middle parts, although the fifth or ninth may occasionally be situated there. The guideline for lowest-note placement should be observed.

- The lead voice is a chord tone or extension.

- The maximum distance between any two adjacent upper voices can be as much as an octave. The root, however, can be separated from the next voice above by as much as a major tenth.

Example 8–6 illustrates sample four-note spread voicings.

In a four-part spread for a triad, a doubling will naturally occur. The root or fifth of the chord is usually the doubled note, although the third can be doubled if it is the root, fourth, or fifth of its related tonic key (Example 8–7).

Example 8–6. *Four-part spread voicings*

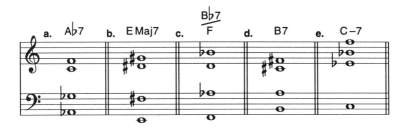

Example 8–7. *Four-part spreads for triads*

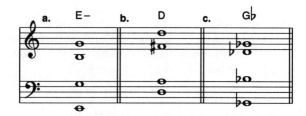

Five Parts

• The bottom note is the root (except for inversions).

• A guide tone is placed in the fourth part. The guideline for lowest-note placement should be observed.

• The third part takes the remaining guide tone and the second part takes a chord tone or extension, or vice versa.

• The lead voice is a chord tone or extension.

• The maximum distance between any two adjacent upper voices can be as much as an octave. The root, however, can be separated from the next voice above by as much as a major tenth.

Example 8–8 illustrates sample five-note spread voicings.

Example 8–8. *Five-part spread voicings*

It is not always necessary for a five-note spread to have five different notes. The lead voice may double one of the other parts (Example 8–9). For the best results when using spreads, it is helpful to work with the practical ranges for each part, as proposed in Example 8–10.

Spreads work best with nonactive, percussive, or independent lead lines. In a progression of spreads, the two middle parts should use basic voice-leading procedure as much as possible—i.e., common tones and movement by step. (See BASIC VOICE LEADING/PIANO TECHNIQUE on pages 69–71). Example 8–11 shows typical spread passages.

Example 8–9. *Five-part spreads with doubling of the lead voice*

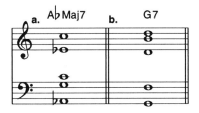

Example 8–10. *Practical ranges for four- and five-part spreads*

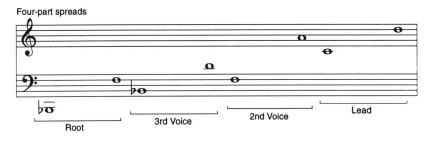

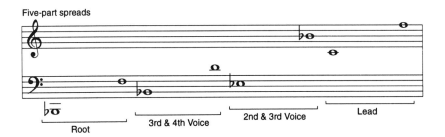

Example 8–11. *Use of spread voicings*

a. Nonactive passage

b. Percussive line

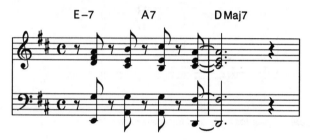

c. Independent lead

CLUSTERS

Clusters are the most compact voicings—here, the principal interval between adjacent notes is the second. *All the notes in a cluster must belong to the underlying chord.* Although the procedures for three, four, and five parts are similar, note the following:

Three / Four Parts
- When there are *three* parts, voicing down from the lead note, all intervals *must* be seconds. With *four* parts, a third can be placed between the two highest voices, when necessary.

- A minor second should not be placed between the two highest voices. However, it is preferable for at least one minor second to be placed somewhere else within the voicing.

- It is not possible to include all the important chord tones, but the basic chord must still be discernible in the resulting structure.

Example 8–12 illustrates sample three- and four-part cluster voicings.

Five Parts
- Voicing down fom the lead note, all intervals should be seconds. A third can be placed within the voicing, if necessary.

- A third or fourth can be placed between the two highest voices.

- A minor second should not be placed between the two highest voices. However, it is preferable for at least one minor second to be placed somewhere else within the voicing.

Example 8–13 illustrates sample five-note cluster voicings.

Example 8–12. *Three- and four-part clusters*

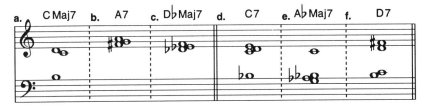

Example 8–13. *Five-part clusters*

For the most effective results when using clusters, it is helpful to work with the practical melody ranges proposed in Example 8–14.

Clusters should not be used in busy or angular passages. They are appropriate for less active, fragmented, or percussive lines (Example 8–15).

Clusters are applicable at both high and low points in passages. On the highest notes in lead lines, clusters intensify the impact of the music (Example 8–16a). On the lower notes of a melody, a cluster may be the best voicing to use in continuing the harmonization (Example 8–16b).

Example 8–14. *Practical lead ranges for clusters*

Example 8–15. *Use of clusters in less active, fragmented, and percussive lines*

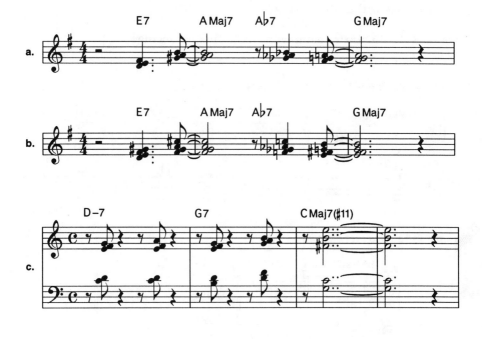

Example 8–16. *Use of clusters at high and low points*

UPPER STRUCTURES

When the three highest notes in a voicing contain at least one extension and form a triad, polytonality results because the upper triad has a root different from that in the primary chord. In this respect the particular melody note in an upper structure, because it is the root, third, or fifth of the triad, determines how an upper structure is completed. Notes from the principal chord should be placed at the bottom of the voicing to support the upper structure.

Upper-structure triads sound nicely when played on the piano. When upper structures are voiced in the horns, however, certain factors come into play. The number and types of horns in an ensemble will determine the completeness of the voicing and the resulting sonority. Generally, because upper structures blend well within the individual families of horns, they can apply comfortably to large ensembles with many horn players. (Upper structures in a large ensemble will be discussed in Chapter 11.) In smaller groups with various combinations of reeds and brasses, an arranger must take care in working with the mixed timbres. Nonetheless, it is possible to create upper-structure voicings with four and five horns, although the possibilities are limited with four parts. Example 8–17 contains sample upper-structure voicings for four and five parts.

Example 8–17. *Upper-structure voicings in four and five parts*

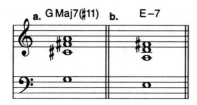

Upper-structure voicings work well highlighting strategic points in passages, particularly high notes (Example 8–18a) or endings (Example 8–18b). Additionally, upper structures are desirable in percussive or fragmented lines (Example 8–18c).

Example 8–18. *Use of upper structures*

a. High points

b. Endings

c. Percussive line

SIX PARTS

A voicing with six different notes uses all allowable chord tones and extensions in the harmony. Six-part voicings are created most easily when configured as or derived from any of the special voicings discussed. It is possible to create resonant six-part voicings in fourths (Example 8–19).

The wide spacing of a spread voicing can easily accomodate six voices (Example 8–20). Although the interior of a spread may be a little more cluttered with six parts, successful results are obtainable.

Example 8–19. *Six-part voicings in fourths*

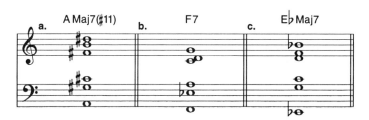

Example 8–20. *Six-part spread voicings*

Example 8–21 illustrates how a somewhat closely spaced voicing can be obtained by dropping two and four in a cluster.

Complete upper-structure voicings are possible with six parts (Example 8–22a). Arrangers will occasionally double the bottom notes of upper structures (Example 8–22b).

Six-part writing should be avoided with faster or active lead lines. As with some of the other special structures, six-part voicings work best in percussive and nonactive passages and at strategic points in phrases. Example 8–23 presents sample six-part passages.

Example 8–21. *Dropping two and four in a cluster*

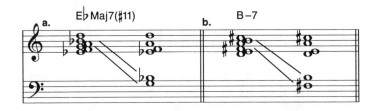

Example 8–22. *Upper structure in six parts*

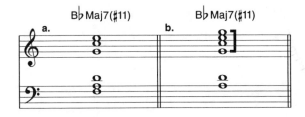

Example 8–23. *Use of six-part voicings*

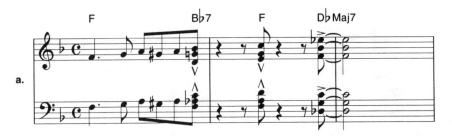

EXERCISES

1. Write out voicings in fourths below the given notes for the specified number of parts.

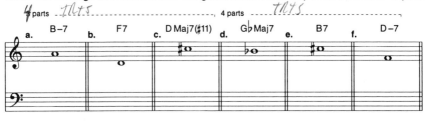

2. Create spread voicings above the given roots for the specified number of parts.

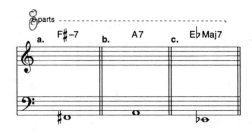

3. Write out clusters below the given notes for the specified number of parts.

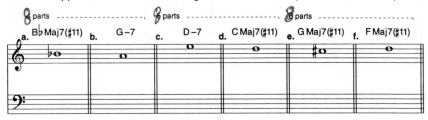

4. Write out upper structures below the given notes for the specified number of parts.

5. Treat the following melody as an independent lead and voice four-part spreads below it.

6. Voice the following melody:
   - a. in five-part voicings in fourths;
   - b. in five parts using any methods but with an
     upper structure on the last note;
   - c. in six parts using any methods.

7. Voice five-part clusters below the following melody.

9

EXPANDED METHODS

ARBITRARY VOICINGS

With the exception of special voicings, the methods outlined in this study have centered primarily around closed structures and how they may be widened by dropping voices. These methods alone, constituting fundamental arranging technique, are enough to produce sophisticated arrangements. With this in mind it is now beneficial to examine other techniques that involve a freer approach. Voicing configurations need not derive from closed voicings; it is possible to be more arbitrary in the spacing of parts.

Spacing

There should be no more than a perfect fifth (though a major sixth is also acceptable) separating any two voices. The lowest voice, though, may be separated from the next-to-lowest voice by as wide an interval as desired. It remains necessary to observe the guideline for lowest-note placement. See Example 9–1 for sample voicings.

Example 9–1. *Voicing considerations for arbitrary voicings*

Five parts: no two upper voices separated by more than a perfect fifth (major sixth); no limitation on distance of lowest voice from next voice above.

Six parts: same considerations; lowest-note placement guidelines must be observed.

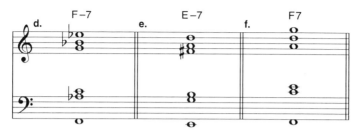

When two inner voices are a second apart, they should not be separated from the adjacent voice, above or below, by more than a fourth (a tritone is acceptable). If, however, the voice below is the lowest voice, the separation can be as wide as desired. Example 9–2 illustrates this principle.

Voice Leading

Some principles concerning voice leading remain constant. An underpart should still have a contour relating to that of the lead line. Ideally, the movement from note to note in an *inner* voice should be the same as that in the melody. That said, voices may occasionally move as much as a major second (even a minor third) more than the lead line at points in a passage It also remains good procedure to aim for contrary motion in at least one part. In addition to these basic guidelines, two other considerations come into play now:

1. Parts may cross.

2. Doublings should be approached and left in contrary motion.

Example 9–3 on page 140 shows passages using the various principles discussed here.

Example 9–2. *Spacing in which two inner voices are a second apart*

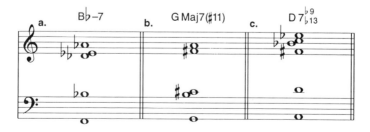

Example 9–3. *Illustrations of voice-leading principles*

a. Seconds not separated from adjacent voices by more than a perfect fourth.

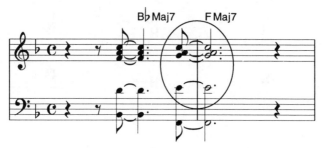

b. Parts may cross.

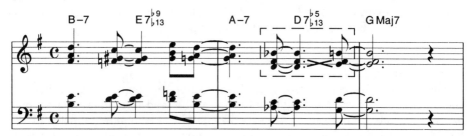

c. Approach and leave doublings in contrary motion.

LINEAR ARRANGING

Linear arranging is a process that incorporates the voicing methods discussed. The linear approach also emphasizes the principles of consonance and dissonance and their relationship to the contour of a musical passage.

Placement of Dissonance

In Chapter 2, the minor second and major seventh were categorized as the most dissonant-sounding intervals. The minor ninth can now be considered the third principal dissonance. *The degree to which any voicing possesses resonance or "bite" relates directly to the number of principal dissonant intervals occurring within its structure.* Example 9–4 illustrates sample voicings that contain principal dissonances.

The strategic placement of dissonance throughout a harmonized passage is the most influential factor in the linear method of arranging. A passage generally contains one or more miniclimaxes leading up to the ending. Consequently, the manner in which a line is analyzed and modified has a significant bearing on the music. In a linear passage an arranger predetermines the location of the specific climactic points. Example 9–5 illustrates how the contours of certain melodies suggest their climactic points.

Example 9–4. *Voicings with principal dissonances*

Example 9–5. *Melodic contours and climactic points*

The next step is to harmonize the climactic points. At the first climactic point it is not mandatory to place a principal dissonant interval in the vertical structure. The manner in which the first point is harmonized dictates how the rest of the passage will be completed. At each subsequent point the amount of dissonance must either be maintained at the same level or increased. In this respect it is important to plan a passage carefully, establishing whether or not to start conservatively. Ultimately, a logical progression of sound quality results; the strongest voicing, one that contains the most dissonance, *ends* the passage. Also, because the resonance of a voicing increases when principal dissonance is lower in the structure, the final voicing in the passage should be the widest. Any available voicing methods can be applied in the harmonizations of the designated climactic points. The following concerns apply:

- Observe the guidelines for lowest-note placement.

- Do not place seconds between the two highest voices *in the climactic points*. (In previous sections, possible uses of seconds between the two highest voices were described—the avoidance of this situation now pertains only to voicings of the designated climactic points when using linear arranging methods).

- Do not place tritones between the two highest voices. (As with seconds, the avoidance of this situation pertains to voicings of the climactic points when using linear arranging methods).

- A third instance of a minor ninth interval between voices is now acceptable: the root of a major seventh chord can be placed a minor ninth above the major seventh.

In Example 9–6, the melodies of Example 9–5 are harmonized at the predetermined climactic points.

Example 9–6. *Harmonizing at climactic points*

a.

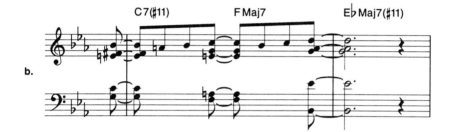

b.

c.

Linking Climactic Points

After harmonizing the designated points in a musical phrase, the next step is to link up the points by adding the lines in between. It is best to complete the bottom line first and then fill in the other parts, usually starting with the second line. A few liberties may be taken *in the lines linking the climactic points* that would normally be avoided in conventional arranging methods:

- Any notes belonging to a chord's scale can be used; also, the guideline concerning lowest-note placement need not apply.

- Seconds and tritones are allowable between the two highest voices; however, consecutive seconds and tritones should be avoided.

- The guideline concerning the separation of seconds from adjacent parts need not apply.

- When the lead line moves, the underparts must also move. Notes should not be repeated in any part beneath the melody.

- The amount of dissonance at any point in a line must either be at the same level or less than that at the approaching climactic point.

In Example 9–7, the melodies that were harmonized at the predetermined climactic points (Example 9–6) are shown with lines added, using the various principles described throughout this chapter.

Example 9–7. *Lines linking climactic points*

In each passage: (1) there is some contrary motion; (2) the widest voicing is at the end; (3) the amount of principal dissonance in the last voicing is the same as or more than in previous voicings.

* At points with asterisks, chromatic approach-note harmonization is used to complete the passage.

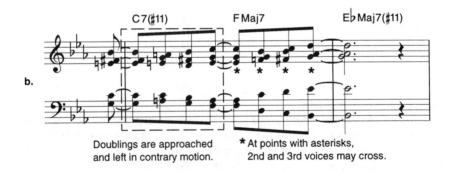

Doublings are approached   * At points with asterisks,
and left in contrary motion.   2nd and 3rd voices may cross.

Encircled notes illustrate that lowest-note placement guidelines need not apply *in the lines.*

Example 9–8. *Use of chromatic notes*

Chromatic notes not belonging to a chord (*not* chromatic approach notes) can be used to improve the movement within a line—e.g., a chromaticism will prevent repeated notes in a part. Resolve chromatic notes by stepwise motion; avoid consecutive chromatics. Example 9–8 contains sample passages in which chromaticisms are indicated with asterisks.

EXERCISES

1. Create arbitrary voicings below the given melody notes for the indicated numbers of parts.

2. Score for five horns using arbitrary voicings.

3. Score for six horns using arbitrary voicings.

4. Score for five horns using arbitrary voicings.

5. Score for six horns using arbitrary voicings.

6. Score for five horns using linear techniques.

7. Score for four horns using linear techniques.

8. Score for five horns using linear techniques.

10

LARGE ENSEMBLES

A band containing more than six horns presents the possibility of forming two smaller combinations within the ensemble that can each be configured in a full chord voicing. (Of course, with seven horns, one subgroup would be voiced in three parts.) In addition, any other subunits voiced in three to six parts might also be formed during the course of an arrangement. Therefore, two keys to arranging successfully for large ensembles are: (1) combining instruments effectively and (2) doubling parts (when desired).

ENSEMBLE WRITING

An ensemble passage occurs when all the horns are playing similar or identical (concerted) rhythms. When the horns are voiced together, certain basic procedures apply. These procedures also constitute the fundamentals of big-band writing that will be examined in the next chapter. Note the following:

1. The brass instruments are at the top of the hierarchy—brasses should be voiced first and then *coupling* (combining) with the saxophones should be determined.

2. Unless a passage is concerted, the saxophones need not move in the same direction as the brasses or they may hold notes while the brasses move—however, the saxes should move only when the brasses move.

3. The saxophones can play notes that are not in the brass parts as long as they are not in conflict with the brass voicings and the harmony in general.

4. Octaves between the brass instruments and saxophones should be approached and left in contrary motion.

Now that these principles have been established, the range of a melody becomes an influential factor in determining how the ensemble will be voiced. With a line that stays within a fairly low range, there are two basic procedures:

1. The brasses are voiced in close position. The saxophones are voiced in the same close position an octave lower (Example 10–1a).

2. The brasses are voiced in close position. The lead saxophone is coupled with the second or third trumpet and the remaining saxes are voiced in close position (Example 10–1b).

Example 10–1. *Melodies within a relatively low range*

With medium- to high-range melodies, the brasses should be voiced closed or one voice, usually the second, should be dropped. The lead saxophone, depending on the number of instruments, plays at or around the second or third brass part and the remaining saxes can be voiced open or spread (Example 10–2).

Example 10–2. *Melodies in medium to high ranges*

a. Concerted passage/parallel motion: brasses voiced closed; saxophones in spreads.

b. Parallel and contrary motion between brasses and saxophones: brasses voiced closed or drop 2; saxophones with double lead voiced closed or drop 2.

COMBINATIONS

The horns in a large ensemble can be grouped into smaller combinations and assigned different functions—e.g., lead lines, counterlines, backgrounds, punches, etc. In these instances it is best that the individual units are scored in a variety of textures. These are again principles that relate also to big-band writing (Chapter 11). Example 10–3 presents sample passages.

Example 10–3. *Use of horns in large ensembles*

a. Saxophones: line in octaves; Brasses: chords in drop 2 and drop 3.

b. Alto and tenor saxophones: melody in octaves; Ensemble: chord punches.

c. Trumpets, Trombone 1, Tenor saxophone: melody in octaves;
Alto saxophones, Trombone 2, Baritone saxophone: backgrounds voiced close or drop 2.

DOUBLING

Logistical or financial factors frequently limit the number of players available for live performances or studio sessions. Consequently, the practice of doubling is significant to an arranger. A *doubler* is a musician who plays more than one instrument. Doublers provide arrangers with extra options for coloring music without having to find extra players. An arranger specifies on the score and on the appropriate part when a player is to switch to another instrument. Experienced doublers are adept at changing instruments quickly. An efficient arranger will have considered in advance the particular instruments involved and the tempo of the music in planning for the switches. As little as a measure or two can be enough time for a player to change instruments.

Doublers can be members of contemporary ensembles of any size. All professional big-band players are doublers (see Chapter 11). In addition to being a useful device for arrangers, doubling can also be gratifying to performers. However, it is important to bear in mind that *a musician may not be as proficient on a double as on his or her primary instrument.* It is obviously beneficial if an arranger knows in advance of the availability and abilities of the doublers.

Woodwind Doubles

A woodwind player can double on one or more woodwinds, often on other members of the same family of instruments. It was pointed out in Chapter 1 that the woodwind instruments are often called reeds; in this respect, woodwind doublers are *reeds players*. In addition to the common woodwinds, some exceptionally accomplished reeds players double on oboe, English horn, bassoon, or other instruments rarely found in jazz bands. However, in most cases it is necessary to employ players who specialize on these instruments. Following is a summary of common situations:

	Possible Double(s)
Saxophone:	Flute
	and/or Clarinet
	and/or Bass Clarinet
	and/or other Saxophone(s)
Clarinet:	Flute
	and/or Bass Clarinet
	and/or Saxophone(s)

It is essential to remember that *the key signature may change when a player switches to a double*—either the new instrument has a different transposition, the arrangement has modulated to a new key, or both of these situations have occurred. Example 10–4 illustrates two passages in which a reeds player switches to a double. Note the indications in writing and the proper notation for such cases.

Example 10–4. *Doubling by reeds players*

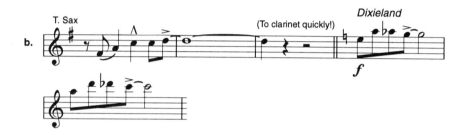

Brass Doubles

Trumpeters frequently double on the flugelhorn. Since the technical demands of the two horns are very similar, an arranger can safely assume that an accomplished trumpet player will be equally proficient on flugelhorn. The cornet is another possible double for a trumpeter, but it is predominantly part of the instrumentation of concert bands.

A trombonist usually concentrates on either tenor or bass trombone. Although some players will own and play both horns, the tenor trombone is the all-around choice in small groups and soloing situations. Some trombonists play the valve trombone, an instrument less widely in use, which has three pistons instead of a slide. Occasionally, a trombonist is also a low-brass specialist who can double on tuba or euphonium (baritone horn). Following is a table of two common situations:

Possible Double
Trumpet: Flugelhorn

Trombone: Tuba

Example 10–5 shows a passage in which a trumpeter is required to switch to the flugelhorn. In this case since the trumpet and flugelhorn are both B♭ instruments, the key-signature change signifies a modulation to a new key in the arrangement.

Example 10–5. *Trumpeter doubling on flugelhorn*

Rhythm-section Doubles

Many bassists play both acoustic and electric instruments. However, a bassist will likely be more proficient on one or the other. Technical demands of the acoustic bass are formidable, and an arranger should not expect an electric bassist to have the same technique on acoustic bass. The same can be true in reverse, although it is more common for acoustic-bass players to double on electric bass with an adequate degree of proficiency.

Although a pianist may double on electric piano or synthesizer, the acoustic piano is the appropriate instrument in pure jazz sessions. The tone and character of the piano are so distinctive and beautiful that it does not make sense to use an electric keyboard in a jazz band unless logistics dictate its use or an arranger desires a specific sound. Electronic keyboards possess features that are appropriate in rock, popular, and commercial music. In any event the acoustic piano can function successfully in all types of contemporary ensembles. An arranger should not assume that an acoustic pianist understands the technical operating procedures of synthesizers.

Most drummers play various other percussion instruments. If an arranger writes a doubling passage for a drummer, it is with the understanding that the drummer will have to stop playing the drum set and possibly change location. In this case an arranger has decided to omit the drum set from the arrangement while the player is doubling. When an arrangement has several percussion parts, one or more players might be added to the ensemble. Following is a summary of common situations:

	Possible Double(s)
Piano:	Synthesizer, Electronic Keyboard(s)
Bass:	Electric Bass
Drums:	Other Percussion

Example 10–6. *Double bass player doubling on electric bass*

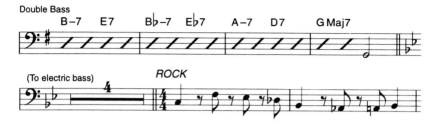

Example 10–6 shows a passage in which a player switches from double bass to electric bass. As in the preceding example, both instruments are pitched identically and the key signature changes only because a modulation has taken place.

EXERCISES

1. Score for four saxes (2 altos, 1 tenor, 1 baritone), two trumpets, one trombone, guitar, piano, bass, and drums.

2. Write a concerted ensemble for four saxes (2 altos, 1 tenor, 1 baritone), two trumpets, and two trombones.

3. Score for five saxes (2 altos, 2 tenors, 1 baritone), three trumpets, two trombones, piano, bass, and drums.

4. Write a concerted ensemble for four saxes (2 altos, 1 tenor, 1 baritone), three trumpets, and two trombones.

5. Write a concerted ensemble for three trumpets, three trombones, and four saxes (2 altos, 1 tenor, 1 baritone).

6. Score for two trumpets and two alto saxes on melody with chords for tenor sax, baritone sax, and two trombones.

7. Score for five saxes (2 altos, 2 tenors, 1 baritone), three trumpets, two trombones, piano, bass, and drums. Have the saxes moving in contrary motion to the brass at some point in the passage.

BIG BAND

The **big band** is the largest ensemble common to jazz performance. This ensemble enjoyed its heyday during the swing era of the 1930s and 40s. Big bands are still part of the contemporary music scene and are almost always included in jazz studies and ensemble programs. Other names for the big band are **stage band**, **dance band**, **jazz ensemble**, and **jazz orchestra**.

INSTRUMENTATION

There is a universally standard instrumentation for the big band. Example 11–1 lists this instrumentation and includes a general synopsis of each instrument's function in the ensemble.

Example 11–1. *Big-band instrumentation*

1st Alto Saxophone *(lead alto)*:
   leads section, ensemble playing, solos
2nd Alto Saxophone:
   section playing, some lead lines, ensemble playing, solos
1st Tenor Saxophone:
   section playing, some lead lines, ensemble playing, solos
2nd Tenor Saxophone:
   section playing, some lead lines, ensemble playing, solos
Baritone Saxophone:
   anchors the section, some lead lines, ensemble playing, solos

1st Trumpet *(lead trumpet)*:
   leads section, high (screech) notes, ensemble playing, solos
2nd Trumpet *(often **assistant lead trumpet**)*:
   section playing, some lead or high notes, ensemble playing, solos
3rd Trumpet:
   section playing, ensemble playing, solos
4th Trumpet:
   section playing, ensemble playing, solos

1st Trombone *(lead trombone)*:
　leads the section, high notes, ensemble playing, solos
2nd Trombone:
　section playing, some lead lines, ensemble playing, solos
3rd Trombone:
　section playing, ensemble playing, solos
4th Trombone (often bass trombone):
　anchors the section, ensemble playing, solos

Piano:
　comps changes, some lead lines, voiced with horns, solos
Guitar:
　comps changes, some lead lines, voiced with horns, solos
Bass:
　bass lines, some lead lines, solos
Drums:
　drives band, solos

Because a big band has complete horn sections—of five saxes, of four trumpets, and of four trombones—it is first necessary to be able to write well for these sections individually before tackling entire ensemble passages. A big-band chart will usually contain passages for a variety of instrument combinations.

SECTION WRITING

A big band's horn sections—saxes, trumpets, and trombines—can play as self-contained units, either alone or in various combinations with each other. Section passages are voiced in harmonies, unisons, or combinations of both.

Saxophone Section

The saxophone section produces a rich, appealing sonority. The saxophones perform melodies, counterlines, backgrounds, and an exciting feature in many big-band arrangements: the saxophone soli. When the five saxes are harmonized as a unit, the usual procedure is to have the first alto in the lead with the remainder of the section voiced below. It is not uncommon to use four-part harmony with the baritone sax doubling the lead line (Example 11–2).

Example 11–2. *The baritone sax doubling the lead line*

Five-part voicings can work, but they will present challenges in faster or angular lines (Example 11–3a). Often, a passage will contain both four-part and five-part voicings at different points—five parts are effective on important punches, chord voicings, slower or held lines, and phrase endings (Examples 11–3b, 3c).

Example 11–3. *Five-part and doubled-lead saxophone voicings*

a. Five-parts.

b. Doubled lead.

c. Combinations.

Although the first alto usually plays the melody in a saxophone soli, other configurations are possible. Example 11–4 shows a soli segment in which the melody range allows the first tenor to be assigned the lead voice. (See also DOUBLING IN BIG BAND on pages 177–180.)

When voicing unison passages for saxophones, two factors are influential: (1) lead range and (2) distribution of the saxophones. The same models should generally play in unison—for example, the two altos (or the two tenors) rarely play in octaves. Any two different saxophone models playing in unison tend to produce a tenor sonority. The five saxophones are rarely voiced in a true unison. Following are further general guidelines:

- Different saxophone models in octaves tend to produce the sound of the smaller model on higher lead lines (Example 11–5a) and the larger model on lower lead lines (Example 11–5b).

- The five saxophones may occasionally be voiced in double octaves (Example 11–5c). In this situation, the highs and lows tend to dominate over the middle.

Example 11–4. *Tenor saxophone in the lead*

Example 11–5. *Unison passages for saxophones*

a. Smaller model saxophone sound.

b. Larger model saxophone sound.

c. Highs and lows dominate.

Trumpet Section

The tone and projection of trumpet sound is as important a factor in big bands as it is in smaller ensembles. Arrangers should plan accordingly when the four trumpets are voiced together as a unit. In general, as long as voicings for the trumpet section are reasonably close and not in the lowest part of the range, the section balance will be good.

With medium-range melodies the four trumpets can maintain adequate control with all but the quietest dynamic markings (Example 11–6).

When the four trumpets are voiced together at the upper end of the range, they add exciting emphasis to a passage. High trumpets are ideal for highlighting important parts of melodies or providing rhythmic punches and background lines (Example 11–7).

Example 11–6. *The four trumpets in medium range*

Example 11–7. *The four trumpets at the upper end of the range*

Range remains an important factor when considering unison passages for the trumpet section. On a melody in the middle to lower part of the range, four trumpets in unison sound well (Example 11–8a). Lead lines in the middle to upper middle ranges lend themselves well to trumpets in unison. If voiced in octaves, it is best to have one trumpet on top with the other three in the lower octave (Example 11–8b). When the four trumpets play a unison line in the higher parts of the range, the sound is intense and will project through the whole band. Place pairs of trumpets in octaves (Example 11–8c).

Example 11–8. *Unison passages for the four trumpets*

Trombone Section

When voicing the four trombones as a unit, the range of the lead line influences the effectiveness of the overall section sound. If the lead line is consistently in the middle to lower part of the trombone's range, a passage of four trombones in harmony can be muddy sounding and cumbersome. Unless a special effect or sonority is desired, the best results occur when the lead trombone is in the higher end of its range. In this case the four trombones produce a well-rounded texture (Example 11–9).

Example 11–9. *The four trombones as a unit*

Unison passages for the trombone section are useful for both melodies and background lines. The guidelines for trombone unison passages are similar to those for trumpet. With a high lead line, the best result is obtained by dividing the trombones into combinations of two and two or one on top and three below (Example 11–10a). On midrange lines, the trombones are voiced in unison. Depending on the tempo and contour of the line, bass trombone can be voiced an octave lower, enriching the texture and providing a strong foundation to the section (Example 11–10b). On low lines, trombones in unison are again a good choice and the resulting sound will be rich and firm (Example 11–10c).

Independent Lead

In Chapter 6, we saw that independent lead writing can be interesting and is often the most logical method to use on melodies that would otherwise be troublesome to harmonize note for note. Example 11–11 illustrates independent lead in each of the big band's horn sections.

Example 11–10. *Unison passages for the trombones*

Example 11–11. *Independent lead for each horn section*

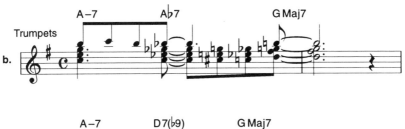

Muted Brasses

Muted trumpets provide a distinctive sonority on melodies and background lines. Because the sound projection is reduced with mutes, one must make sure the lead line in a *harmonized* passage is high enough to allow all the parts to come through (Example 11–12).

Muting all the brass instruments provides interesting sonorities. Following are some common and practical ways in which the muting can be distributed among the brasses:

1. All brass instruments use cup mutes or plungers.

2. Trumpets are muted differently using straight and cup mutes as opposed to trombones which use cup mutes only.

3. Some brass instruments are muted and others are open.

As pointed out in Chapter 1, arrangers must plan charts accordingly so that players have time to insert or remove mutes. Example 11–13 shows passages for muted brass.

Example 11–12. *Muted trumpets*

Example 11–13. *Muted-brass sonorities*

SECTION AGAINST SECTION

Individual elements—melodies, counterlines, backgrounds, ostinatos, etc.—can be assigned to individual horn sections. In this manner sections retain their identities when combined in a passage. It is important to strive for variety and to make sure the various elements are discernible. For instance, if there is an active lead line in a passage, the background or counterline might be relatively inactive or a succession of held notes. Also, all sections should not be voiced alike, except in unisons. Various configurations are possible:

- Two or all three of the horn sections are in unisons.

- Two of the horn sections are harmonized; or one section is harmonized and one other section is in unison.

- Two horn sections are in unisons and the remaining horn section is harmonized.

- Two sections are harmonized and the remaining section is in unison.

In Example 11–14, the trumpets play the melody partly in unison and partly harmonized; saxophones and trombones are harmonized. The three sections do not *step on each other*—saxophone and trombone figures supplement the trumpet line and move when the melody holds.

Example 11–14. *Section against section: trumpets playing the melody both in unison and harmonized*

Example 11–15. *Section against section: baritone sax voiced with trombones*

The baritone saxophone sometimes functions independently of the other saxophones, usually interacting with the trombone section. (Example 11–15). When the fourth trombone is at or near the low end of its range, the baritone sax may double it. When the fourth trombone is playing higher notes, the baritone sax will often play below it and add "bottom" to the sonority.

ENSEMBLE WRITING

As with other large groups, a big-band ensemble occurs when all the instruments are playing similar or identical rhythms. The brasses are again at the top of the hierarchy, and the shape of a passage is dictated by how the brasses and saxophones are coupled. Although rhythm-section instruments are occasionally part of the ensemble passage, they will usually continue to perform their basic functions or occasionally lay out.

Basic Procedures

The basic methods for big-band ensemble writing are identical with those discussed for large ensembles in Chapter 10. The difference now is that there are several more horns to add into the mix. With lead lines of limited activity and narrow range, denser voicings and a somewhat freer approach may be applicable. In any event *do not place the lead alto saxophone at or above the level of the lead trumpet.* There are two basic procedures:

- Trumpets are voiced in close position; the trombones are voiced in close position an octave below. The lead alto saxophone doubles the lead trombone and the other saxes are voiced in close position (Example 11–16a).

- The brasses are voiced in close position. Saxophones are voiced in a more open position and the lead alto saxophone should be at or below the second trumpet part (Example 11–16b).

Example 11–16. *Basic ensemble writing for the big band*

Concerted Writing

Active, wider ranging lead lines require that all parts move identically—concerted writing (Example 11–17). It is also better to stick to basic four-part harmonies. The lead alto saxophone again should not be written above the second trumpet part.

Rhythmic and percussive lines with a fairly narrow range lend themselves well to higher degrees of dissonance. Voicings should increasingly widen in descending from top to bottom. The tension should be placed in the high brasses in closed position. Low brasses plays basic chord sound, mostly roots and fifths, in open voicings. The saxophones should also be voiced open, the bottom two or three usually in unison with the low brasses (Example 11–18).

Example 11–17. *Concerted writing*

Example 11–18. *Ensemble writing: percussive figures*

Shared Lead

Lead lines can be shared in two principal ways:

1. among different sections in the original register

2. among different sections with octave displacement at different points.

Example 11–19 shows a melody in its original design and three instances in which it is shared among the sections of the big band.

Example 11–19. *Sharing the lead*

Original melody.

a. Any of these melodic segments can be doubled at the octave below.

b. Any of these melodic segments can be doubled at the octave below.

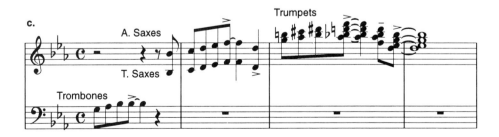

UNISONS

When many instruments play the same line, the sonority is thick and dynamic. From a creative standpoint an arranger can choose unison writing for its impact. In a practical sense, a unison, like an independent lead, is sometimes the best way to treat a melody that would otherwise be difficult to harmonize. Consequently, an ensemble unison depends upon melodic strength and instrument location. In this respect melody ranges can be wider than usual since an arranger does not have to work out chord voicings.

Whether the melody is in a high or medium range, the instruments are usually placed in double octaves. On high melodies two or three trumpets are placed on top; alto saxes, the remaining trumpets, and two or three trombones are in the middle; and the remaining trombones and baritone sax are on the bottom. The tenor saxes are "swing" voices that can play in the middle or on the bottom, depending on the range of the part. If possible, separate the tenor saxes. Example 11–20 illustrates an ensemble unison on a high melody.

On medium-range melodies, the instruments will not not be split up as much. Place the instruments in their strongest ranges (Example 11–21).

Example 11–20. *An ensemble unison in high range*

Example 11–21. *An ensemble unison in medium range*

Example 11–22. *A rare true unison*

Although a true unison is possible for the full big band, it rarely occurs. The melody would have to be of narrow scope, not ranging too far away on either side of middle C. Occasionally, when a darker sound is desired, or when a few notes are too high to allow a true unison by all the instruments and when the passage is not too active, the trombones and baritone saxophone may play an octave lower (Example 11–22).

CHORDS

Saxophones and Trombones

Saxophones and trombones blend well in chords. Because the alto saxes are are always on the highest notes, the lead note in the voicing should not be too low. Following are basic procedures:

- The alto and tenor saxophones are voiced in close position and the trombones are voiced close an octave below; the baritone saxophone plays beneath the fourth trombone, usually adding the root or fifth of the chord (Example 11–23a).

- The alto and tenor saxophones are voiced in close position and the trombones are voiced open; the baritone saxophone doubles the fourth trombone (Example 11–23b).

- The alto saxophones are the two highest voices and the tenor saxophones couple with the two highest trombones—when the fourth trombone is playing relatively high, the baritone sax may add another voice below it; on low bottom notes, the baritone saxophone either doubles the fourth trombone or the bass trombone may play below the baritone saxophone (Example 11–23c).

Example 11–23. *Saxophone and trombone chords*

Brasses

When the eight brass instruments are voiced in a chord, the trumpets are placed above the trombones. Following are basic procedures:

- Both sections can be voiced in close position with the trombones an octave below (Example 11–24a).

- The trumpets are voiced in close position and the trombones are voiced open (Example 11–24b).

The trumpets remain in close position in both situations because they lose their homogeneous texture the wider they are spread in a voicing.

Example 11–24. *Chords for all eight brasses*

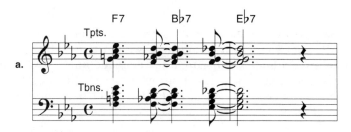

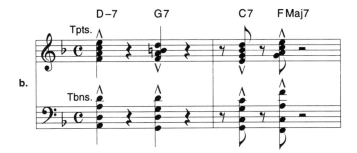

Upper structures sound particularly well in the brass. Trumpets play the upper triad and the primary chord is given to the trombones (Example 11–25).

Full Big Band

When voicing chords for the entire big band, the procedures are similar to those examined in ensemble writing. Once again, the brass are at the top of the hierarchy. Some doublings may occur, usually at the lower end. Chords for the big band vary in loudness and dissonance, depending on the range of the lead note and the musical context. There are few sounds in contemporary music that match the intensity and excitement of a full-blown big-band chord with lead trumpet screeching at the end of an arrangement. Example 11–26 illustrates some chord voicings for the big band.

Example 11–25. *Upper structures in the brasses*

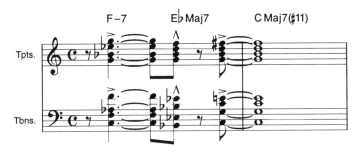

Example 11–26. *Full-blown big-band chords*

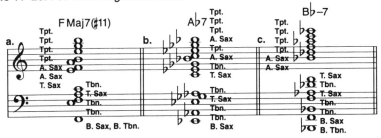

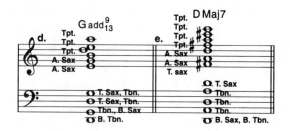

DOUBLING IN BIG BAND

General doubling practices were outlined in Chapter 10. In a big band the situation is somewhat different in that each horn player is generally expected to play specific doubles. With reeds players, the saxophone is, as usual, the primary instrument, and it should be considered a player's strongest horn. Following is a summary of doubles for big-band horn players:

	Usual Double(s)
1st Alto Saxophone:	Flute and/or Clarinet and/or Soprano Saxophone
2nd Alto Saxophone:	Flute and/or Clarinet
1st Tenor Saxophone:	Flute and/or Clarinet and/or Soprano Saxophone
2nd Tenor Saxophone:	Flute and/or Clarinet
Baritone Saxophone:	Flute and/or Bass Clarinet and/or Clarinet
Trumpets (all):	Flugelhorn
4th Trombone:	*Possible Double* Tuba

Doublers in a big band automatically provide an opportunity for alternative instrumental colors and combinations. An arranger needs only a rich imagination to create passages for various mixes of primary instruments and doubles. Passages can also be written for complete sections of doubles—e.g., for five clarinets including the bass clarinet, for five flutes, for four flugelhorns, etc. It is naturally impossible to determine or illustrate every doubling combination. A few representative examples should provide a good idea of how doubles can be used effectively.

Two or more clarinets voiced together provide a rich, reedy sonority. Example 11–27 presents sample passages.

Two or more flutes voiced together sound nicely on melodic material and as backgrounds (Example 11–28a). When the range permits, flutes often double the lead line an octave above the trumpets (Example 11–28b).

Example 11–27. *Clarinet sonorities*

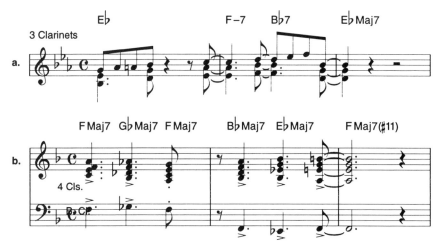

Example 11–28. *Flute sonorities*

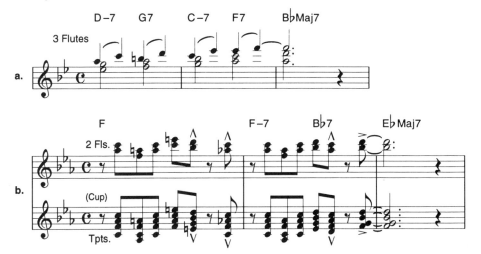

Flutes and clarinets in combination can be used effectively, either performing principal melodic material or background lines (Example 11–29).

The soprano saxophone is frequently assigned the lead role in a saxophone section (Example 11–30). The soprano lends a distinctive sonority to the section and may be used for the complete duration of a chart rather than being treated as a double.

The flugelhorn has a more rounded sound than the trumpet and is an excellent brass choice to play melodies when a plaintive or serene mood is desired. (Example 11–31).

Example 11–29. *A flute and clarinet combination*

Example 11–30. *A soprano-saxophone lead*

Example 11–31. *A flugelhorn melody*

Example 11–32. *Use of doubles*

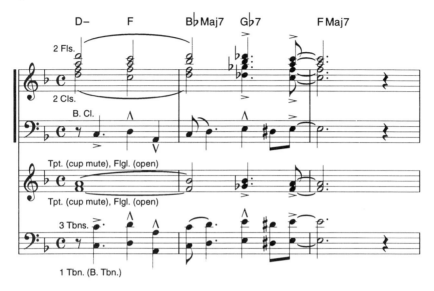

In addition to their melodic and sectional capabilities, doubles provide interesting colors in chord voicings. The high woodwinds can be especially effective. Example 11–32 illustrates a passage for big bands in which most of the doubles are voiced in a chordal background behind a melody performed by the bass clarinet and trombones.

HORN AND TUBA

The horn and tuba are regular members of orchestras, classical chamber ensembles, and concert bands. They are not commonly associated with small jazz and popular groups, though there are always a few jazz players on the scene who are excellent technicians and soloists on their instruments. Where the horn and tuba do flourish are in arrangements for large ensembles. Although they are not part of the standard instrumentation in a big band, or even common doubles, they are potentially appealing additions because of their distinctive sounds and colors.

Although other musicians of the time were also experimenting with non-conventional instruments in jazz settings, the earliest notable use of the horn and tuba was in Miles Davis's ensemble for his historic *Birth of the Cool* recording in 1949. *Cool jazz* reflected a more intellectual and compositional approach to the music. The amalgamation of jazz and classical compositional methods and instrumentation that, in turn, grew out of cool jazz became known as ***third stream*** music. Gunther Schuller and Gil Evans, two classically trained and influential composers, were the significant collaborators with Davis. In the years since, Anthony Braxton has been the most proficient and recognized player/composer to straddle the worlds of jazz and classical music. In general it behooves arrangers to write for the horn or tuba only when they know in advance that the instrument(s) will be included in the ensemble of a specific project or engagement.

As pointed out in Chapter 1, the horn has a range of almost four octaves and, except for the highest and lowest areas, is quite flexible. The horn has an appealing, noble sound when performing melodies (Example 11–33a); it also blends well in ensemble passages (Example 11–33b).

Example 11–33. *The role of the horn*

The tuba, in spite of its large size, can be both an agile and melodious instrument in the hands of an accomplished player. Its full, rounded sound allows it to blend nicely in ensemble or low brass passages (Example 11–34a). In addition, the tuba functions well, as might be expected, as a foundational voice in sustained passages, punches, and chords (Example 11–34b).

Example 11–34. *The role of the tuba*

a. Ensemble

b. Foundation

EXERCISES

1. Score for five saxophones (2 altos, 2 tenors, baritone), piano, bass, and drums.

2. Score for four trumpets, piano, vibraphone, bass, and drums.

3. Score for four trombones, guitar, piano, bass, and drums.

4. Score four five saxophones (2 altos, 2 tenors, baritone), four trombones, piano, bass, and drums.

5. Score for four muted trumpets, four muted trombones, piano, bass, and drums.

6. Score for big band: 5 saxes, 4 trumpets, 4 trombones (including bass trombone), guitar, piano, bass, and drums.

7. Score for big band (including bass trombone) with 2 horns and 1 tuba added to the instrumentation.

8. Voice chords for full big band below the given lead trumpet notes. Do each example twice: First with standard big-band instrumentation (without bass trombone); and then with 2 horns and 1 tuba added to the big band (this time with bass trombone).

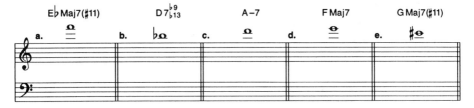

9. Score for four clarinets and bass clarinet.

10. Score for three flutes, clarinet, and bass clarinet.

APPENDIX 1: SCORE AND PARTS

Score

Example A1–1. *The first page of a score*

The first page of a score always shows the complete instrumentation of an arrangement. Instruments are spelled out in full; abbreviations are used from the second page on.

concert-pitched score

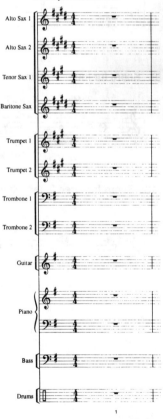

transposed score

On every page of a score, the sections within the ensemble are highlighted by a thick line, brace, or bracket on the left side of the score. In the scores on this page, the saxophones are obviously one section.

The baritone sax and tenor sax are sometimes notated in the bass clef in a concert-pitched score. The transposed parts for both saxes are always in the treble clef.

The trumpets and trombones are grouped as separate sections in these scores; they could also have been grouped in the scores as one brass section. In any case scores should be labeled clearly, as shown.

The guitar is notated identically on concert-pitched and transposed scores. The guitar sounds an octave lower.

The bass is notated identically on concert-pitched and transposed scores. The bass sounds an octave lower.

Drum parts are notated with a percussion clef.

On contemporary scores the measures are individually numbered, most often to the left or centered below the bottom staff.

Example A1–2. *Standard instrumentation for big bands*

This is the universally standard instrumentation for big bands—illustrated in both concert and transposed scores. If horns and tuba are added to the instrumentation, the horns are placed between the trumpets and trombones, and the tuba is placed below the trombones.

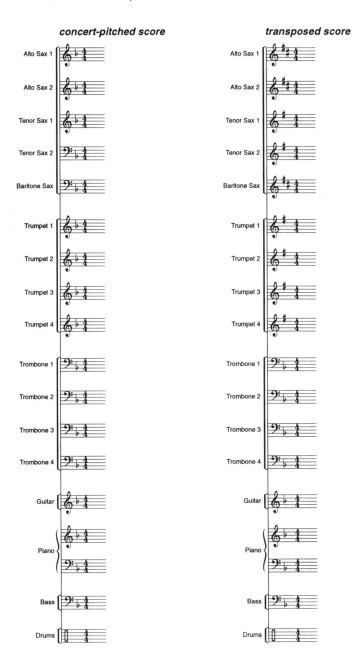

Example A1–3. *The first page of a big-band score*

First page of a big band score: (1) Title centered above; (2) Composer/arranger indicated at top right; (3) Instruments listed in full; (4) Written directions at top of score; (5) Measures numbered to left or centered below the lowest staff.

© 1997 Norman David

Example A1–4. *After the first page*

From the second page on in a score, instrument abbreviations are used. Enclosed rehearsal numbers (sometimes letters) are placed above the highest staff at important points in the arrangement.

Parts

Example A1–5. *A part copied out from a score*

Parts are extracted (copied out) from the score and transposed when necessary. A part includes everything in the score pertaining to it—meter, tempo, dynamics, articulations, solos, etc. The trombone part shown here appears as it would on a score because the trombone is a nontransposing instrument.

Trombone 1

THIS MUST BE IT

composed & arranged by Norman David

Example A1–6. *The part of Example A1–5 transposed up a major ninth*

The part shown in the preceding example is presented here again, this time transposed up a major ninth to be playable by a large-model B♭ instrument. Note that the key signature and soloing chords are also transposed up a major second to be playable on a B♭ instrument.

Tenor Sax 1

THIS MUST BE IT

composed & arranged by Norman David

APPENDIX 2: THE ARRANGER'S TOOLS

As with all creative-arts activities, arranging is a personal expression. Everything that goes into an arrangement—voicings, chords, articulation marks; dynamic and phrasing indications; intros, codas, soloing sections—reflects the insights, sense of organization, and daring that the arranger experienced when writing the chart. The care and emotional attachment to one's arranging work should be as intense as they would be with music composition or performance.

The materials available to an arranger and the environment in which his or her work is carried out are significant factors. Until the last quarter of the twentieth century, the image of a composer was that of a dedicated individual hunched over the piano keyboard with pencil in hand pondering the next few notes. For composers and arrangers, or just creative music enthusiasts, the image was alluring, symbolic of a world that only a limited number of people ever visit. The single event that would forever alter the image, as it would in virtually every other vocation in the world, was the invention and refinement of the personal computer.

Arrangers can now conceivably produce a completed work without even picking up a pen or pencil. Sophisticated software and technology related to the computer make it possible to carry out countless musical functions by simply pressing keys or pushing buttons. Although this last statement may seem an oversimplification, it actually contains a large element of truth. In any event, regardless of the wonders of computer technology, an arranger must still be schooled in the theory and practice of music—then he or she can decide whether or not to push buttons. Beautiful manuscripts can be produced either by hand or technological means.

Music Pens, Pencils, Papers

Before computers, the final drafts of arrangements were done primarily in ink using music pens with specialized *nibs*. This remains a viable and widely used method that requires skill and experience. Nibs come in many shapes and sizes; anyone who uses pens will have personal equipment preferences. Nibs can be *straight* (contact is made at a 90° angle to the paper) or *oblique* (a 40° angle); points can be fine, medium, or broad. Inks specifically created for music writing are available for use with the pens. It is also necessary to use high-quality papers that are compatible with ink and reproduce well.

Another method for copying music that has been common for a long time is that of writing with pencil, or pen, on special papers made of *onion skin* (often called *vellum*). These papers, on which neat and damage-free erasing is possible when using pencil, are suitable for high-quality reproduction. For many years, the primary reproduction method used with onion skin papers was the *ozalid* process, in which a specialized machine would produce black print copies from the onion-skin pages. Clean and legible penciled drafts can also be duplicated excellently with professional photocopying. More conventional papers can, of course, be used with pencil; they will also reproduce well. However, care must be taken in the initial drafts since excessive erasures can damage the paper's surface.

A drawback when using commercially produced papers is that the spacing and sizing of staves, systems, and even the full page cannot be adjusted. Also, severe notational errors often are extremely difficult to rectify despite the availability of products such as correction fluids and adhesive strips. The handwritten work of an accomplished copyist represents true artistic craft; an arranger who chooses to write everything by hand must have as firm a grasp on copying methods as on the technique of arranging.

Many music stores sell or can order the various music paper and handwriting materials that are available. There are also several companies, mostly in New York or Los Angeles, that provide music copying and reproduction services. Many faculty members or students at music conservatories and college music departments will usually be able to recommend efficient private copyists or alternative but capable copying services. George Heussenstamm, in *The Norton Manual of Music Notation* (see complete citation in the Selected Bibliography), presents an excellent and thorough discussion of traditional notational techniques and reproduction processes; he also provides addresses for some of the bigger music-reproduction companies.

Computers: Hardware and Music Software

As alluded to, the computer has dramatically created new possibilities in all aspects of music creation. Both IBM-compatible and Macintosh platforms can accomodate much of the available software—however, Macintosh generally has the upper hand in music applications. This is essentially due to the fact that Macintosh is more user-friendly with respect to the sophisticated music software programs that continue to crop up. Many software developers, aware of this, are developing their top-of-the-line products with the Macintosh platform in mind. In both the huge industry of commercial music production and the major field of movie-soundtrack composition, Macintosh is predominant. Whatever the case, an arranger who opts to use computers obviously will choose his or her system of preference.

An emerging technology that undoubtedly will have yet another great impact on the music industry is a program that will enable handwritten music to be *scanned* (photographed for reproduction) and converted to the format of music-notation software. This is an exciting technology—as long as the handwritten music is reasonably legible, an arranger can attack a project zealously without being overly concerned about erasures or total neatness. When the music is transferred onto the screen, the software will make it visually presentable and permit accurate proofreading and revising. For those musicians (like the present author) who rue the gradual disappearance of things traditional, the evolving technology can nonetheless be appealing and can allow for the best of both worlds—one can still experience the uniquely human sensation of mind cooperating with body that would come with physical handwriting; the important yet often tedious phase of editing and error checking can then be carried out on the computer.

However anyone looks at it, the professional music-notation software that is available is extremely useful, multifaceted, and in the unwavering process of becoming the status quo. Software producers are designing sophisticated programs to meet every need. Literally, thousands of *fonts* have been and continue to be developed. There are even jazz fonts available that look exactly as if they were handwritten by professional copyists. Another invaluable asset of computer technology is that paper can be designed and printed to exact specifications for individual projects; once a score format is created, it can be stored and printed again whenever needed. Arrangers and composers can now present their work in state-of-the-art printouts, often produced using the same equipment and software as used by professional publishers.

With any of the computers or software available, it is essential to have good printing capabilities. Print technology, as with the other computer-related technologies, is significantly advanced and some excellent printers are available. The output of a printer is measured in *d.p.i.* (dots per inch). For most basic printing needs—such as letters, memos, or flyers— 300 d.p.i. will suffice. However, personal printers come in reasonably affordable 600 d.p.i. models that are well worth the investment; music printed on these more advanced models will have noticeably sharper definition. While various print technologies provide satisfactory results, *laser* printers will furnish the most professional-looking manuscripts.

BIBLIOGRAPHY

General Reference and Analysis

Gerow, Maurice, David Megill, and Paul Tanner. *Jazz*, 8th ed. Dubuque, IA: Brown & Benchmark, 1997.

Gridley, Mark. *Jazz Styles*, 6th ed. Upper Saddle River, NJ: Prentice-Hall, 1997.

Kernfeld, Barry, ed. *The New Grove Dictionary of Jazz*. London: Macmillan, 1988.

Martin, Henry. *Enjoying Jazz*. New York: Schirmer, 1986.

Megill, Donald and Richard Demory. *Introduction to Jazz History*, 4th ed. Upper Saddle River, NJ: Prentice-Hall, 1996.

Wheaton, Jack. *All That Jazz!* New York: Ardsley House, 1994.

Instrumentation, Arranging, Orchestration, Composition

Adler, Samuel. *The Study of Orchestration*. New York: W. W. Norton, 1989.

Baker, David. *Arranging and Composing for the Small Ensemble*. Van Nuys, CA: Alfred, 1985

Blatter, Alfred. *Instrumentation/Orchestration*. New York: Schirmer, 1980.

Bruner, Tom. *Basic Concepts of Arranging and Orchestrating Music*. Pacific, MO: Mel Bay, 1993.

Burton, Steven. *Orchestration*. Englewood Cliffs, NJ: Prentice-Hall, 1982.

Delamont, Gordon. *Modern Arranging Technique*. Delevan, NY: Kendor Music, 1965.

Dobbins, Bill. *Jazz Arranging and Composing: A Linear Approach*. Rottenburg, Germany: Advance Music, 1986.

Hansen, Brad. *The Essentials of Instrumentation*. Mountain View, CA: Mayfield, 1991.

Kennan, Kent and Donald Grantham. *The Technique of Orchestration*, 4th ed. Englewood Cliffs, NJ: Prentice-Hall, 1989.

Miller, Ron. *Modal Jazz Composition and Harmony*. Rottenburg, Germany: Advance Music, 1992.

Piston, Walter. *Orchestration*. New York: W. W. Norton, 1955.

Rinzler, Paul. *Jazz Arranging and Performance Practice: A Guide for Small Ensembles*. Metuchen, NJ: Scarecrow, 1989.

Russo, William. *Jazz Composition and Orchestration*. University of Chicago, 1988.

Sebesky, Don. *The Contemporary Arranger*. Van Nuys, CA: Alfred, 1984.

Shatzkin, Merton. *Writing for the Orchestra: An Introduction to Orchestration*. Englewood Cliffs, NJ: Prentice-Hall, 1993.

Music Notation

Casale, Sammy. *The Art of Music Copying and Basic Notation*. Pacific, MO: Mel Bay, 1993.

Heussenstamm, George. *Norton Manual of Music Notation*. New York: W. W. Norton, 1987.

Roemer, Clinton. *The Art of Music Copying*. Sherman Oaks, CA: Roerick Music, 1984.

Stone, Kurt. *Music Notation in the Twentieth Century*. New York: W. W. Norton, 1980.

Contemporary Theory

Gordon, Christopher. *Form and Content in Commercial Music*. New York: Ardsley House, 1992.

Lawn, Richard and Jeffrey Hellmer. *Jazz: Theory and Practice*. New York: Alfred A. Knopf, 1996.

Levine, Mark. *The Jazz Theory Book*. Petaluma, CA: Sher Music, 1995.

Reeves, Scott D. *Creative Jazz Improvisation*. Englewood Cliffs, NJ: Prentice-Hall, 1989.

Sorce, Richard. *Music Theory for the Music Professional: A Comparison of Common-Practice and Popular Genres*. New York: Ardsley House, 1995.

INDEX